Attides

Birmingham

26.1.85

NEW STREET
REMEMBERED

NEW STREET REMEMBERED

The Story of
Birmingham's
New Street
Railway Station
1854-1967

Donald J Smith

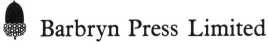 Barbryn Press Limited

British Library Cataloguing in Publication Data

Smith, D.J. (Donald J.)
New Street Remembered: the story of
Birmingham's New Street Railway Station
1854-1967.

1. New Street Station (Birmingham) — History
I. Title
385'.314'0942496   HE3019.B5

ISBN 0 906160 05 7

First published in 1984 by Barbryn Press Ltd
37-38 Calthorpe Road, Birmingham B15 1TX

© Donald J.M. Smith & Barbryn Press Ltd. 1984.

Photoset by Advertiser Printers Ltd., Newton Abbot and printed in Great Britain by Streetly Printing (Birmingham) Ltd.

Contents

Introduction

New Street, Birmingham, has always been the largest railway station in the second city and one of the most important outside the London area, but has received far less publicity than many stations half its size. This book is an attempt to record something of the history and atmosphere that survived from the pioneer days of railways to its replacement by the present modern structure.

It superseded a neo-classical building designed by Hardwick known as Curzon Street, about a mile distant to the south east. This was the northern terminus of the London and Birmingham Railway Company, into which several minor companies had running rights. The first major trunk route, known as the Grand Junction Railway, brought a line from the Liverpool and Manchester system to a temporary station in the Vauxhall suburb of Birmingham, north of Curzon Street, opened in 1837. This proved inadequate and, after the opening of Curzon Street in September 1838, most traffic from the north was diverted to the new terminus via a specially constructed loop.

As the railway system developed in the West Midlands and nation-wide, running rights into Curzon Street were also obtained by the Birmingham and Gloucester Railway from the south west and the Birmingham and Derby Junction Railway from the north east, these companies eventually merging to become the Midland Railway Company.

From 1st January 1846 the Grand Junction and the London and Birmingham Railways merged to form the London and North Western Railway, known for many years as the 'Premier Line'. One of the first aims of the new company was to build a much larger through station on a site nearer to the commercial and administrative centre of Birmingham than either Curzon Street or Vauxhall. This was shared with the Midland Railway Company and several other groups, either under the aegis of the Midland Railway or the 'Premier Line'. They included the Birmingham, Wolverhampton and Stour Valley Railway, vested in the L.N.W.R. in 1867.

The South Staffordshire Railway, serving Walsall and joining the former Grand Junction main line at Bescot, was also absorbed by the L.N.W.R. in 1867. The North Staffordshire Railway had extensive running rights into New Street but remained independent until the grouping of 1922, when it was absorbed into the newly-formed London, Midland and Scottish Railway. The Harborne Railway was a semi-independent line, opened in 1874 and closing—to passenger traffic—in 1934. The Birmingham and West Suburban Railway was a small system on the south west side of Birmingham, terminating at Albion Wharf, absorbed by the Midland Railway in 1875. The main line of the latter system was eventually used as a more convenient access to what became the Midland side of New Street Station and part of the main route between Bristol and Leeds.

Sunlight & Shadow. A view of the LNWR side of New Street Station that offers a wonderful sense of atmosphere. Probably taken from platform 2, looking south east.

Birmingham Post & Mail

7

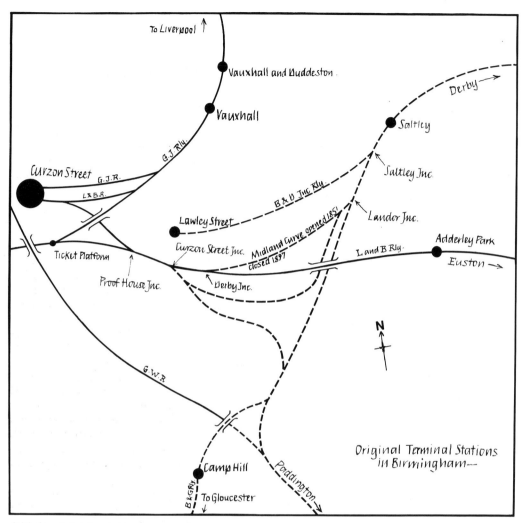

Original terminal stations in Birmingham 1850.

1.
The First Station

With the amalgamation of the main line companies involved, and threatened incursions from a recently approved Stour Valley line, a new station in Birmingham was essential. It was soon a matter of public interest and civic debate where this should be and which groups allowed development rights. There were, by the mid-1840s, two main arteries of traffic extending from south east to north west, intersecting near the heart of Birmingham.

The London, North Western Railway (the self-styled 'Premier Line') and the Great Western Railway were chief contestants in these disputes. Although the Midland Railway eventually absorbed the short Birmingham West Suburban line, the Stour Valley line was always under the aegis of the L.N.W.R.. Certainly the Premier Line owed the Midland Company a debt of gratitude for foiling attempts of the Great Western to monopolise the Birmingham and Gloucester route and convert it to broad gauge throughout. It was not at first conceivable that rival companies should enjoy equal prosperity or share the luxury of two enlarged through stations.

A site nearer the centre of Birmingham within fifty or sixty yards of New Street was eventually considered the chief goal of the L.N.W.R. Snow Hill, (later to become the main Great Western Station) also entered the controversy but was considered less attractive as a workable commercial proposition. An Act of Parliament passed into law on the 3rd August 1846, granted authority for the L.N.W.R. to build at New Street. This had been approved by Robert Stephenson, then also surveyor to the Stour Valley line, who claimed that New Street might soon become an 'exact model of the Manchester and Leeds Station in Manchester'—which, due to restrictions at Curzon Street, had overtaken the Birmingham depots, to become the busiest in the world.

An important stipulation of the New Street Act ensured that if a station were to be built on the site there would be a public right of way through the main buildings to compensate for the possible elimination of King Street and Pleck Lane. This was to be a short cut between the upper and lower parts of the town, or from the administrative and business quarters to the market centre and a busy manufacturing district. The privilege guarded by the Act has been maintained and respected to the present day, although pedestrians now pass above rather than through the station, where there is a precinct of shops with an extensive concourse, having escalators to the lower level of the main entrance and booking hall. The Act stated that such a passage must be kept open for all time, which is a different matter from remaining open all the time. It was necessary — as a legal safeguard — to close the passage one day in each year, while during the First World War use was restricted on Sundays to bona fide railway passengers. By the late 1890s, 80,000 people used the passage each day, including both passengers and ordinary pedestrians.

9

The overall Act of 1846 had been prompted as a result of numerous public and committee meetings, also by a parliamentary investigation concerning the needs of local railways, including those of the Stour Valley line and the Great Western Railway. Regarding station sites, various conflicting claims had been made before a select committee, at which Robert Stephenson among others had been invited to give evidence.

At a meeting of Birmingham Council there was a vote of 16 to 6 in favour of New Street, a former Mayor, Alderman Weston, claiming that "New Street was more central with easier approaches than Snow Hill", although — taking into account the greater flow of traffic in New Street — these statements tended to be contradictory. John Lord, described as a general merchant, claimed that "All buildings of any note were in the neighbourhood of New Street", although this was a far from accurate observation even in those days. It was, however, generally agreed that "business was continually leaving the Snow Hill area", although no-one then claimed that such a trend might be reversed by building a large railway station, as eventually happened.

Support for New Street came from an unexpected quarter as the headmaster of Birmingham Free School (later known as King Edward's Grammar School), then occupying a site in New Street, thought that even a railway station would prove a better neighbour than the slum dwellings and small taverns then surrounding his establishment. The old Free School would have overlooked the New Street site from the southern end, at what would have been the throat of the station. It was described as a 'handsome building' in the Gothic revival style designed by Sir Charles Barry, although backed by cramped cottages and noisesome workshops that were a nuisance to the school.

Charles Shaw, a local business magnate and Birmingham magistrate, known to have share-holdings in the Oxford, Worcester and Wolverhampton Railway, later absorbed into the Great Western Railway, voiced strong objections to New Street in the name of public order. He claimed that New Street had gone down in the world and was one of the most dangerous and undesirable spots in Birmingham, where extra police were always on duty to prevent riot and guard both life and property. It was a known meeting place for law-breakers of all types, while pickpockets were rife.

The Building of New Street Station

The task of building New Street Station commenced with the opening of a short line from Curzon Street, approximately a mile in length. This section of track was laid under the L.N.W.R. (Birmingham Extension) Act of 1846, and cost £35,000, a modest sum even for those days. There was a tunnel at the northern end of the extension, 273 yards long, later incorporated into the south tunnel.

Before construction could begin there had to be a programme of intensive demolition. The part concerned was mainly old and dilapidated property and although the street commissioners had previously grumbled concerning changes in more respectable quarters, they were eager enough to see the end of such rookeries.

The main entrance to New Street Station was to be near the junction of Navigation Street with Lower Temple Street. For a short period it was termed 'Navigation Street' and even the 'Grand Central Station', assuming the title of 'New Street' with the opening of Stephenson Place, which served as a short cut from the main thoroughfare about 60 yards distant, becoming an unofficial driveway to both the station and Queen's Hotel.

Land acquired for building included a quarter known as the Froggary (an unsavoury network of courts and alleys), Pleck Lane, Little Colmore Street and King Street, all of which were reduced to rubble. It was to make up for the destruction of Pleck Lane (in particular) that a pedestrian way and footbridge were built across the station, eventually used by large numbers of people, in preference to other routes, as it was also a covered walk. Three nonconformist chapels or places of worship were included in the demolitions, known respectively as 'The Chapel', 'The Welch Chapel' (where Welsh services were held for the large Welsh-speaking community of those days) and the Lady Huntingdon Church, used by the Countess of Huntingdon's Connection, forming a splinter group of the Wesleyan Movement. The first Birmingham Synagogue and the old prison-house in Pleck Lane were also swept away.

George & Robert Stephenson. Robert (right) was the engineer-in-chief of the London and Birmingham Railway, assisted by his father.

~George Stephenson 1781–1848   Robert Stephenson 1803–1859~

Pulling-down and almost total rebuilding took seven years and cost over half a million pounds, demolition work starting in 1846. Part of the land and property used belonged to the Grammar School or old Free School and was bought from the Board of Governors for £39.000. This did not affect the main school buildings which were eventually perched on a cliff of masonry at the southern end of the station at least 50ft above rail level. Throughout the period concerned only two hundred men were at regular work on the site at any given time.

The Stour Valley line was opened two years before the completion of New Street, this including the building of Monument Lane Station, where it first terminated, and later the north tunnel — which brought the line into New Street from the north west. Trains ran through from Wolverhampton some time before the official opening, using what was described as a temporary or side platform. A single through carriage was run from Wolverhampton each day and sent on to Curzon Street, where it was attached to a London express. The mile long stretch of track between Monument Lane and New Street was opened on the 1st July 1852.

For a short period New Street served as a terminus only, the first train to enter the station coming off the Stour Valley line. The Midland Railway was invited to share the station with extensive running rights, but in the role of tenants, until a change of plan in 1897. This arrangement was a sequel to use made by the former Birmingham and Gloucester Railway of Curzon Street, covered by Acts of Parliament. Proprietary rights were vested in the L.N.W.R., while the M.R. was charged a nominal rent, but with a share in working costs and general expenses.

Curzon Street, in 1840. The station master's house on the right.

New Street was officially opened for trains, both north and south, on the 1st June 1854. The opening ceremony, in keeping with the ideals of the L.N.W.R., was brief and dignified. Many of the magnates and higher officials of the L.N.W.R. and M.R. were present, plus a deputation from the town council. There was also the opening at New Street of the first telegraphic signalling in the district, first used for controlling trains through the tunnels from the Grand Junction Box at the south end, and from Sheepcote Lane Box — near Monument Lane — at the north end. Up to that time telegraphic communications functioned only between some of the larger towns, with many smaller places, including most villages, without such a convenience. Before this innovation — on the railways — trains not arriving within twenty minutes of their schedules were hunted-out by a search party on a light engine.

In a letter to the *Birmingham Post* dated 11th February 1931, a Mrs J. Cameron of Coventry claimed that her husband's father, while still a youth, was the first guard on a train out of New Street after the official opening. At that time John Cameron junior, as he was then, had been a pupil at the Free School in New Street, where he had taken an interest in the construction work from an upper window. While visiting the house of a friend, he expressed a forlorn wish that he might be the guard on one of the first trains to leave the new station, never dreaming that such a thing might happen. A stranger, who appears to have been an official of the railway company, and overhearing the remark, was able to grant the wish, John being appointed a temporary guard, 'just for the day'. He was also given a specially designed cap with the figure '1' embroidered above the peak, and was nominally in charge of the first passenger train to leave the station.

At the time of opening there were four through platforms and four traverser or turntable roads. According to a ground plan of the 1860s the platforms were designated, from the New Street side, in the following order: Two bay platforms on the right (entering New Street from Stephenson Place) for Stour Valley departures and a pair of bay platforms on the left for Midland Railway departures. Continuous platforms east to west, had arrivals from Liverpool and other northern cities, with departures for London and the south on the left. Two through tracks divided the station almost in half with Midland and South Staffordshire arrivals on left and right, directly opposite the above. Departures for Liverpool and the north, plus arrivals from London and the south, were on an island platform also shared with Midland and South Staffordshire arrivals, while a further departure platform for the same destinations backed on to Great Queen Street (not to be geographically confused with a much shorter Queen Street, on the other side of the station) later becoming the Queen's Drive.

The railway approaches to the station were through long tunnels, further spanned by road bridges at both ends. At the north western end were the Hill Street and Navigation Street bridges, with a Worcester Street bridge spanning the opposite approaches. Navigation Street was so-named as it terminated opposite the main basin and offices of the Birmingham Canal Navigation Company.

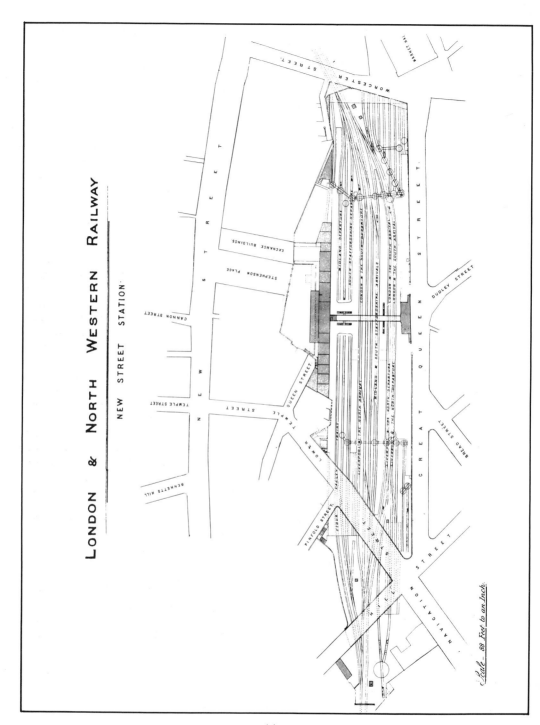

LONDON & NORTH WESTERN RAILWAY

NEW STREET STATION

Scale - 88 Feet to an Inch.

14

There were eventually twenty-six small turntables providing access between running lines and sidings for items of four-wheeled stock, frequently man-handled or horse-hauled in the station area. At the Hill Street-Navigation Street end there was also a locomotive turntable able to cope with the largest tender engine then in use. At this early period the public right of way ended near the station entrance from Great Queen Street, opposite an oblique junction with Dudley Street. Flights of steps leading to platform level from the pedestrian-way were in pairs facing each other on opposite sides of the public footbridge. The sides of both bridge and steps were of cast iron lattice or strap-work with iron treads, based on an iron framework but with bronze hand rails. The first flight down on each side led to a small landing from which there was a change of direction back towards the footbridge, ending at platform level. People who remembered the station in its earlier days claimed that the original footbridge was much higher and narrower than in later years, also more exposed.

With a later programme of modernisation and an increase in passenger movements during the 1880s the steps were found to be dangerous, also likely to slow-down general mobility. Narrow steps were replaced by a broader, safer structure, again two flights on each side but with larger half-way landings and both flights in one direction only. Side panelling was introduced to protect both the steps and parapets of the footbridge, while there were also strip advertisements on the risers of each step in the form of enamelled signs. Numerous posters and enamelled-iron signs eventually lined the footbridge and its approaches.

An open signal cabin, later surmounted by a double aspect clock, was erected on girders above the footbridge between platforms one and two, reached by means of a vertical ladder and trapdoor. There were rounded arches above the heads of each stairway to platform level, with the number of the platform displayed on a roundel supported in turn by a shank or spindle of cast iron, facing at right angles to the platform and towards oncoming pedestrians. Space on the arches was eventually utilised, as on the parapets, for crude advertising purposes.

There were eight elegant gaslit standard lamps in the centre of each platform, four on each side of the footbridge.

This was essentially a passenger station, although with facilities for loading and unloading horses and road vehicles, also for coping with milk traffic, fish, parcels, newspapers and luggage deliveries — all associated with passenger stock. New Street was recorded in the official guide of the Railway Clearing House as a passenger and parcels station able to deal with furniture vans, carriages, small portable-engines, horse boxes and prize cattle vans. It may be noted that horse-drawn furniture vans or pantechnicons were taken to the station by a team of horses, then run on to a flat carriage-truck of a passenger train, to be met at the station of its destination by another team, hired in advance.

Through goods or mineral trains were rarely seen at New Street, except the odd train on Sundays or as the result of diversions necessary because of repairs or accidents. These latter were improbable if not impossible, as there were several bypass routes, with circular lines or layouts enclosing the outer

Ground plan of New Street Station (LNWR) during the early 1860s.

15

suburbs. The diversity of routes referred not only to the Birmingham area but to the West Midlands as a whole.

There had been two lock-up shops on the bridge since the 1880s, directly opposite each other, near the steps leading to the original platform three. The one on the left from the New Street side was a high-class tobacconist frequently displaying hand-made pipes in the window, while on the right there was a confectioners known as the Bridge Candy Shop, or Stores.

Description of New Street Station at the Time of Opening.

The exterior of the main entrance, on the New Street side, was a form of arcading with ten rounded arches of dressed stonework. The upper and main structure was of grey stock-brick, having string-coursing of stonework between storeys and stone quoining (cornering) also known as long-and-short-work. A balustrade above the upper or fourth floor guarded the pitch of a shallow roof, serving as a parapet, above which two further storeys were added during the 1900s.

Wings on either side of the central block, the ground floor of which was the main booking hall, were three storeys high, eventually forming part of the Queen's Hotel. The wings were slightly recessed from the arcading to a depth of double arches of which only the outer and slightly larger arch was accessible. The furthermost wing and arcading faced on to a spacious forecourt narrowing at the Navigation Street end — to the width of two vehicles. This was slightly lower than Stephenson Place, which also fell from the direction of New Street proper. A short road, at right angles to Stephenson Place, continuing to a junction with Lower Temple Street and Navigation Street, was later known as Stephenson Street. Double gates of elaborate wrought ironwork, flanked by stone pillars of massive construction, each pillar topped by a tall iron-lamp, guarded the carriage entrance from Stephenson Place. Foot passengers were expected to use side or wicket gates across the pavements.

There was a lodge-like building, sometimes serving as an enquiry or excursion office, on the right of the gates, and a screen of railings extending in parallel with the entire frontage. Each rail was 14ft high, topped by a gilt fleur-de-lis, as though guarding the Bastille. The gates were seldom used, at least during the present century, and removed for scrap metal during the Second World War. During the 1900s the railings were replaced by bollards and the low retaining wall — formerly beneath the railings — by wooden-sheathed steps. Thomas Cook had a busy office almost opposite the main carriage entrance. Hard-by the later enquiry office, also near the entrance gates, was an agency for the Shropshire Union Railway and Canal Company, an undertaking later merged with the L.N.W.R.

Along the Stephenson Street side of the railings, at the slightly higher level, was a cab rank. There was also a much shorter rank in Stephenson Place, and, until the 1900s, a cab rank and cabman's shelter on the Navigation Street road bridge. Two or three hansom cabs or four-wheelers were sometimes allowed to wait inside the railings but the carriage drive was normally reserved for private vehicles.

While the internal layout of the station was planned by Robert Stephenson and his assistants, the external buildings and those on the frontage were designed by an architect, J. W. Livock. Platforms and tracks of the interior were covered by an arched roof of single span, constructed of glass and iron. This had a length of 840ft, a span of 212ft and maximum height, from ground level, of 80ft. Construction began in 1852 while William Baker was the Chief Engineer of the L.N.W.R. On completion, it held the world record for the largest single-span roof ever made. Although St. Pancras was eventually wider it was also 29ft shorter. Design and overall planning of the roof was the domain of engineer E. A. Cooper (1819-1893), who had previously worked on the design of the Crystal Palace. There were 115 tons of glass and 1,400 tons of iron sheeting in the domed part alone. It was described as a crescent-truss roof, made up of 36 trusses, each truss being 45 tons in weight. The trusses were mainly of wrought iron with smaller members of cast iron, on columns of cast iron. After the collapse of a similar but smaller roof at Charing Cross Station in 1905, numerous steel tie bars were added as a safety measure.

The massive columns and their entablatures, which supported the roof were made by the Ketley Blast Furnaces of Kingswinford, near Stourbridge. The capitals or heads of the columns were cast separately. The major part of the ironwork was supplied and erected by Fox, Henderson and Company, of London Works, Smethwick, this being one of the firm's last contracts before they failed in 1853 and went into liquidation. Glass covered an area 120,000 square feet, while iron-sheeting accounted for 100,000 square feet. Total area covered was 4 acres.

The public footbridge, in September 1885. Note the departure board across the bridge.

National Railway Museum.

Business letter on LNWR-crested notepaper. Queen's Hotel 1896.

Bryan Holden Collection.

Part of the frontage of the Queen's Hotel, showing one of the domes added in 1917.

Birmingham Central Library.

18

The ponderous members were raised into position by means of a travelling stage, working from end-to-end of the station area. Between the ribs and pillars was an ingenious system of rollers and bearings which allowed for expansion and contraction due to atmospheric changes. The ends of the station roof were screened-off to the level of the lowest horizontal tierods, using fluted glass supplied by Messrs Chance Bros. It was planned to continue the roof to the Navigation Street bridge but further extensions were to be of ridge and furrow design. The last members were fixed on the anniversary of the day when the first pillar was set-up. Despite its weight and area, 'with almost cathedral-like splendour', the whole was said to have 'a light and elegant appearance', at least until disfigured by the grime of half a century.

> According to a report in the *Illustrated London News* for June 3rd, 1854 . . . "Entering the station by an arcade we first arrive at the booking offices . . . and passing through these emerge on a magnificent corridor or gallery guarded by light railings . . . from whence broad staircases with bronze rails afford access to the departure platform. We then stand on a level with a long series of offices, appropriate to the officials of the railway company, and a superb refreshment room about 80ft long and 40ft broad, divided into three portions by rows of massive pillars. We must ask the reader to imagine that he stands on a stone platform $1/4$ mile long; that behind him lies a range of massive pillars projecting from the station wall, that in front of him are ten lines of rails, four platforms and a broad carriageway. Let him add to this that he stands amidst the noise of half a dozen trains arriving and departing, the trampling of crowds of passengers, the transport of luggage, the ringing of bells and the noise of two or three hundred porters and workmen, and he will have a faint idea of the scene witnessed daily at the Birmingham Central Station."

The Queen's Hotel.

The hotel part of the building, incorporated with the frontage of the station, was also designed by William Livock. It was opened at the same time as the official opening of the station in 1854. There were eventually nine hotels under the control of the L.N.W.R., with the Queen's Hotel, New Street, recognised as the second largest and most important. Its telegraphic address was "Besthotel Birmingham". Trains were frequently met by hotel porters in distinctive red jackets, by whom luggage was carried to and from the hotel free of charge, although tips were appreciated. Railway company porters, wearing ordinary uniforms, were not allowed to cross the threshold.

The original entrance from Stephenson Place was on the left of the arcading, until later changes and extensions. This was an arched doorway flanked by flattened Doric columns in the form of a portico, its inner steps rising to a reception area or foyer. A sculptured or free-standing version of the L.N.W.R. coat-of-arms (later removed) was mounted on a plinth directly above the doorway. The pavement area in front of the portico was patrolled by a cockaded and liveried carriage attendant, armed with a large umbrella, especially in wet or blustery weather. There was also a direct entrance from the station on platform one.

19

QUEEN'S HOTEL BIRMINGHAM.

NEW STREET STATION, BIRMINGHAM.

The hotel had restaurants open to both residents and non-residents, several bars, a grill-room, smoke-rooms, a coffee-room and over sixty suites with bedrooms, dressing rooms and private sitting rooms, apart from public rooms. It was furnished at the height of contemporary fashion and appears to have become a meeting place, on a social level, for both businessmen and persons of leisure. Dinners and lunches could be ordered from both table d'hôte or à la carte menus, while afternoon teas — of great elegance and variety — were offered between three thirty and five p.m. It was *de rigueur* for both sexes to dress for dinner, except in the grill-room. Prices, by any standards, were reasonable.

Four years after its opening the hotel was leased by the L.N.W.R. Company to its resident manager — a Mr Scott. From 1872 it was renamed the North Western (Queen's) Hotel, to prevent this title being adopted by a rival establishment on the opposite side of Stephenson Street, later to become the Midland Hotel, although not having direct connections with either railway company. The name 'Queen's and North Western Hotel' appeared from the mid-1870s in elegant lettering above a row of sash windows of the second storey. At the time of opening the whole building was covered in layers of stucco, but after considerable cracking and patching-up this was entirely removed.

Entrance to the LNWR side of New Street and the Queen's Hotel from Stephenson Place. Note the attempt to grow trees in the forecourt. Circa 1870.

Mrs Una Bradbury Collection.

In 1911 the hotel was re-acquired by the L.N.W.R., reverting to its original name. During this period the impressive main entrance ceased to be used by the hotel and the coat-of-arms removed. A new doorway was on the right of the arcading, flanked by cant bay windows, there being two bays on the left and three on the right. Two large towers were built at each end of the frontage, topped by pepper-pot domes. A common balcony joined all second floor rooms, but appears to have been mainly decorative. Further changes and improvements were made during 1917. These included the addition of two extra stories and a new wing or extension at the Navigation Street end. Accommodation for both guests and staff was then doubled.

The main dining room was on the ground floor to the right of the new entrance, forming part of the frontage, and remarkable for the beauty of massive crystal chandeliers. Kitchens were in the basement beneath the dining room, from which savoury odours of soup and entrée wafted through an area guarded by low railings. Supplies were transferred from street level to basement on a manually operated lift at the end of the building, usually worked by a youth wearing the traditional uniform of a hotel page, his short tunic or shell-jacket covered with rows of silver buttons. For many years a similar lift supplied foot-warmers to a distributing centre on platform one, at the rear of the hotel. One of the functions of the hotel kitchen was to supply restaurant cars, on certain long distance trains with partly cooked joints of meat and roast fowls that merely had to be reheated and finished.

Platform 3 from the southern end, showing siding to the carriage loading bay in foreground. Note wagon turntable and shunting horse on right. Circa 1896.

Mrs Una Bradbury Collection.

From 1911 a glass canopy of new art design, in leaded lights, projected above the porch, also bearing the name of the hotel. There were swing and later revolving doors presided over by a uniformed commissionaire with burnished medals. Reservations for rooms could be made free of charge by telegram or telephone from any point on the L.N.W.R. or the Caledonian Railway. For this to be done it was only necessary to contact a station official or guard of the train on which the would-be guest was travelling. The telephone number was Central 5531. The hotel was recognised as four star rating by both the R.A.C. and the A.A.

There was universal admiration for both station and hotel throughout the Midlands and at national level. After a short period it outstripped the prototype in Manchester recommended by Robert Stephenson, both statistically and as a centre for modern enterprise. Banks, shops and offices were soon opening in close proximity, while other hotels and restaurants attempted to rival, if they could not surpass, the North Western (Queen's) Hotel.

The Midland Station.

The Midland Railway, although working at New Street in harmony with the London and North Western, must often have felt the desire for their own station and room to expand. As traffic increased over both systems there was a need for greater development that eventually doubled the station area to become a joint rather than a shared depot, with two separate but connected buildings under unified control. A joint-tenancy dates from 1897 when the Midland were at last freed from the indignity of regarding the L.N.W.R. as its patrons and superiors. From this year until the major regrouping in 1923, each railway chose an overall manager or station superintendent for alternate years, backed by a joint committee with equal representation for both companies.

New Street Station, Midland side, platform 4, looking south. September 1885.

National Railway Museum.

22

To build the new part of the station more run-down property was purchased at the rear of the L.N.W.R. building. This was mainly on the opposite side of Queen Street, where work began in 1883. Among the demolitions, which covered part of Dudley Street, were a few business premises, many terraced cottages, a small church and an extensive burial ground. When the church was demolished bodies from the graves and vaults were removed to a reserved plot at Witton Cemetery. A new church building located in Bristol Street, paradoxically known as the 'Old Meeting Church', was constructed as a replacement. Station developments further covered an area of waste land frequently used by hawkers and cheap jacks as an open market.

According to an official guide to the Midland Railway, published in 1884, in a mention of New Street . . . "we are surrounded by the bewildering bustle of a station which, although one of the largest in the country, and indeed in the world, is about to be considerably enlarged."

The Midland Extension, as it was then termed, opened in February 1885, the first new platform coming into use on the 8th of the month. Eight months later the full working pattern was established and north east to south west expresses were entirely diverted to the new building. From the mid-1880s the L.N.W.R. operated platform numbers 1, 2 and 3, which consisted of two up and two down main line platforms and five bays. The Midland were responsible for platforms 4, 5 and 6, with two up and one down main lines and one bay. Total area was $14\frac{1}{2}$ acres with 8 acres covered over. The Midland part of the station cost half a million pounds.

Platform 2 looking north-east. The locomotive on the middle road is an LNWR (rebuilt) 'Bloomer'. Note the loading gauge on the right and windows of the Queen's Hotel overlooking platform 1.

National Railway Museum.

23

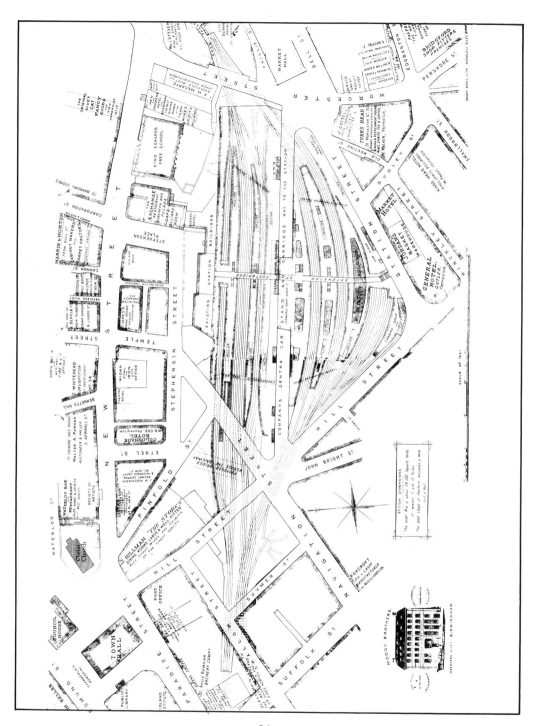

24

Work involved in demolition and reconstruction affected not only the layout of the railway but the pattern of surrounding streets, which now assumed the ground plan remaining until the vast reorganisation of town planning during the 1960s. The meandering length of Great Queen Street was converted to a broad, straight carriage drive, while to the north of the station a much narrower and truncated Queen Street had already disappeared, replaced by an improved Stephenson Street. A footway between ordinary shops and the Midland Hotel — known as Burlington Passage — plus a passageway between the Colonnade Hotel and the Theatre Royal, with the short vehicular thoroughfares of Temple Street and Ethel Street, all made for easier contact between New Street and Stephenson Street or the station and the upper part of the town.

There were now subways at both ends of the buildings, eventually connecting all platforms and the sorting office of the General Post Office in Hill Street, about a quarter of a mile distant. These underground passages were approached down a series of ramps, from platform level, the entrances protected by barriers of ornamental ironwork with prominent gaslamps. They were forbidden to passengers, except in emergencies, and reserved for trollies, barrows or hand-carts used in the transfer of luggage and mailbags. Frequently spaced notices advised passengers to 'cross by means of the footbridge only.' There were also lifts for some of the heavier barrows that could not be pushed up the slopes when fully loaded. Lifts, ramps and underground passageways were completed by the late 1880s.

The overall plan of both stations formed a basin-shape, although the base, as if in the hands of an unskilled potter, was slightly off-centre. The top or L.N.W.R. side was fairly straight while the Midland or underside had a curved profile. In consequence the main block of the Midland buildings conformed to this curvature. It was bounded — for almost its entire length on the south west side by a new road known as Station Street. Opposite the station, sites were occupied by the Market Hotel (extant), Jordan's Basket Warehouse and the General Hotel. It was in this row that Birmingham's first Repertory Theatre — the nursery of many international stage and screen stars — was opened, about thirty years later. High brick walls with ridged coping stones and deep insets or panels, surrounded the Midland buildings, screening them from the traffic of Station Street and Hill Street. The Midland entrances for passengers, also connecting with the public footbridge, were under a glass roof, curved downwards at the Station Street end to resemble a palm house or conservatory at a country mansion. There was also a more direct and separate entrance leading to the footbridge, which bypassed the booking hall. A covered cab rank and vehicle parking area on the left of the main entrance, turning into Station Street, was guarded by double iron gates.

Ground plan of combined LNWR and MR sides at New Street, as from the mid-1880s. The total station area was about twelve acres, and the length of platforms exceeded one and a half miles.

Another gateway, equally impressive, almost at the junction of Lower Hill Street and Station Street, led into a loading bay for carriages, with a parallel fish dock, collectively known as the 'back sidings'. The loading bays and cab ranks were mainly under glass roofs, fanning out on both sides of the central passenger entrance. These latter were supported by uprights, girders and

New Street Station, Birmingham.

"Scott" Series No. 232.

The northern end of the Queen's Drive, showing the overall roofs. The LNWR side is on the left, extended towards the Navigation Street bridge in the form of ridge and furrow construction. Circa 1896.

T Nicholls Collection.

diagonal cross-members on the ridge and furrow plan, also used in other parts of the buildings, especially spanning the Queen's Drive near the footbridge. The Midland train shed had overall protection from twin-arched roofs of glass and sheet metal, that survived the world wars and post-war deroofing of the L.N.W.R. side. These were known as 'Paxton' roofs, as they resembled the structure of the Crystal Palace, designed by Sir Joseph Paxton for the Great Exhibition (Hyde Park) in 1851. They could be described as twin but minor versions of the L.N.W.R. roof, also depending on elborate roof trusses. While the L.N.W.R. roof, was straight the twin-roofs of the Midland side were of a curved or crescent-shaped ground plan. Glass on both sides was partly removed, as a safety measure, with the outbreak of the Second World War.

The main booking office on the Station Street side, at one time exclusive to the Midland Railway, was of a bowed or semi-circular ground plan, at the foot of steps leading on both sides to the upper level of the footbridge. Above the several ticket windows were instructions for travel and bookings to Gloucester, Cheltenham and Bristol. Tickets for Sheffield, Leeds and points north east were more frequently procured from a booking office approached at two levels — either from the footbridge (known to railway staff as the 'bridge') or from the Queen's Drive, leading on to platform four. There was a similar two-level booking office on the L.N.W.R. side of the Queen's Drive, opening on to platform three. There were several large wooden buildings, especially on the Midland side.

Midland architecture was not perhaps as impressive as the L.N.W.R. frontage, lacking the majestic facade of the neo-classical Queen's Hotel. General design evinced a more homely approach to the classical style, its main recognisable feature being a curved pediment, with deep mouldings, directly above the Station Street entrance, penetrated by a circular or bull's-eye window. The general effect was dominated by glass roofs and curtain walls of the forecourt, most parts of the structure being almost invisible except from the upper windows of opposite buildings.

Station Street often had the impression of being even busier than Stephenson Street, as the large forecourt was missing on the Midland side, which acted as a syphon for all but limited through traffic. Apart from ordinary traffic to the nearby retail and wholesale markets, there was also a street tramway and later numerous bus shelters.

There was access to a Midland Railway Parcels Office in Station Street, near the junction with Worcester Street and the Queen's Drive. A London and North Western Parcels Office, also a recruiting centre for railway staff, was just inside the driveway, but on the opposite side of the road. The surface of Station Street, in common with the Queen's Drive, was cobbled with square setts, the slightly raised edges of these giving dray and van horses a better chance of purchase when coping with heavy loads, especially as the gradient rose steeply towards Worcester Street and the Market Hall.

The Queen's Drive was one of the most impressive parts of the new developments, which continued on a minor scale well into the 1890s. It occupied the former side of Great Queen Street, as previously mentioned, neatly dividing the Midland and North Western sides. Where the drive was

Entrance to the Queen's Drive at the southern end, opposite the Market Hall. The MR parcels office is on the left and the LNWR parcels office on the right.

Birmingham Central Library.

spanned by the public footbridge there was a covered section over the head of a cab rank controlled by the railway companies, with entrances directly on to the nearest platforms from either side of the drive. There were broad pavements on both sides and impressive double gates at each end, closed for legal purposes, on one day in each year. Gates at the south eastern or Worcester Street end opened near a road junction, almost a crossing, between Station Street, Bell Street and Worcester Street.

At the opposite or north western end of the drive, which dipped towards the centre, there were further ornamental gates, the vertical bars of their metalwork intertwined with the initial letters of the controlling companies. The north western gates officially opened into Navigation Street at a busy junction with both Hill Street and John Bright Street. Trams and buses made extensive use of Navigation Street but could not proceed into Stephenson Street and Stephenson Place, which gave the Queen's Hotel a measure of comparative privacy, at least on one side.

A contemporary author, J. Pendleton, writing in *Our Railways,* published in 1896, commented, "New Street Station presents the most vivid picture of swift go-ahead life of the city (Birmingham). The traffic has grown so rapidly that it has become absolutely necessary for the L.N.W.R. to improve the approaches, to double one south tunnel and put down additional lines... What improvements and extensions will be necessary in the next quarter of a century it almost passes the wit of railway engineers to conceive..."

Improvements mentioned concerned elevation of main running lines between Proof House Junction and the tunnel exits to span the Curzon Street approaches, this being on the south eastern side of the station. The extra height gave passengers entering Birmingham from the south a glimpse of the interesting Georgian Proof House (where locally made gun barrels are tested), on the facade of which has been carved a colourful 'trophy of arms', in the heraldic style of the late 18th century. This track improvement was completed and brought into daily service on the 7th May 1893. Midland trains to the north east now left the area of New Street via a burrowing junction that commenced under the Queen's Drive, traffic from both the L.N.W.R. and M.R. sides able to leave Birmingham without crossing on the level. A short time before these changes were made there had been a collision in which an M.R. locomotive and train had rammed the side of an L.N.W.R. train at an acute angle, fortunately without serious injuries.

In the *Birmingham Post* for the 3rd January 1896, it was announced that the last part of the south tunnel was now complete, forming a tube through the heart of Birmingham that required five million bricks for the open retaining walls alone. The Birmingham West Suburban tunnel between Five Ways and New Street had been opened in 1885. The seven tunnels leading into New Street have always been very difficult to negotiate, at both ends of the station, on curves or with the need for banking. Lines in the western direction rise dramatically from the platform ramps, trains also having to encounter a maze of pointwork almost immediately. Regular banking commenced on the Midland side in 1914. During wet or slippery weather ashes were frequently strewn on the tracks.

Because of the public right of way it was almost impossible to check tickets of people leaving and entering the station and no platform tickets were issued until the rebuilding of the mid-1960s. Trains bound for New Street, apart from certain expresses and those with travelling ticket collectors, were stopped at various stations for inspections to be made, managed with the minimum loss of time. Collectors boarded the trains at Monument Lane, Vauxhall and Adderley Park on the L.N.W.R. lines and at Saltley, Camp Hill and King's Norton on the Midland lines. Sometimes an inspection was made in the trains at New Street or as a 'snap check' at the head of the stairs leading on to the platforms. The staff involved were always polite and cheerful men, neatly dressed and sporting flowers in their button-holes, sometimes hothouse blooms, which were given them by regular passengers, either connected with floristry or having private greenhouses.

In general terms the Midland Railway was slightly more efficient and friendly than the L.N.W.R. Midland coaching stock — according to several reports — were frequently carriages that were more up-to-date and comfortable than vehicles on the Premier Line. The Midland may certainly have been rich and powerful, but the London, North Western with its even longer traditions and aristocratic connections was more aloof, autocratic and self-assured. It made far more noise than the Midland, with louder and more imperious whistles, those of the so-called 'Crew pattern' known to be ear-splitting. The blasting-off of certain engines has been described by R. T. Coxon, in his book on *Roads and Railways of Birmingham–1900-1939,* as 'like an infernal organ recital'.

Although not greatly increasing noise levels, while adding a touch of weird charm, shunters (especially on the Midland side) made signals on instruments resembling hunting horns. Each horn of copper or brass would be tapered to the mouthpiece and about a foot in length, being half curved. Due to restrictions of space some of the shunting movements carried through into the tunnels, where warning signals were made by bells or gongs, worked by hand levers. Shunters were on duty day and night, in shifts, operating the levers, blowing horns and keeping in close touch with the signalmen in their boxes.

Stories of Old New Street.

In sifting through files and cuttings on the subject of New Street Station during the Victorian era, there are numerous interesting stories from officials retiring after periods of long service with the railway companies. These offer many revelations concerning manners and modes, not only in one of the major industrial cities of Europe but in the day-to-day running of a large main line station.

Many courting couples or old friends and fellow travellers were said to have met in the arcade at the front of the station, also near a large table or luggage rest in the booking hall at the top of the steps, on the New Street side, which was removed in 1892. "Meet me at the top of the steps" or "by the table' were familiar sayings of those early days. The space occupied by the table was later filled by vending machines — mainly penny-in-the-slot types, dispensing chocolate-bars and luggage tags.

In the pre-motor days this was the hub of Birmingham, the bridge frequently jammed with all types of people from every corner of Britain and its Empire. Among the crowds were often those with household names in statecraft, commerce, industry, the arts and national affairs. Prominent citizens such as the Wilkinsons, Nettlefolds, Cadburys, Martineaus and Chamberlains made frequent use of the station, especially in their contacts with London. Late one night Joseph Chamberlain, the cabinet minister and Conservative statesman, thundered down Stephenson Place in his carriage and pair, hoping to catch the 00.50 am for Euston. On alighting he was told the train had "just gone out" so adjusting his top hat and famous eyeglass he entered the station superintendent's office and ordered a special train, hinting at large tips all round if this could be arranged at so late an hour. The morning papers announced, in banner headlines, "Capture of Dr. Jameson" — which started a chain of events leading to the war in South Africa. "Thus" it was said "do Colonial Secretaries have their peaceful nights disturbed."

Many famous actors and actresses came to Birmingham via New Street and crowds of women and younger people waited for hours to see the arrival of their favourite stars. Henry Irving and Ellen Terry were among the most popular of these, often appearing in Birmingham theatres. The crowds were so eager and demanding that such V.I.P.s had to be escorted to their carriages by a squad of railway police, the latter still wearing their top hats and tailcoats long after they had been discarded by the city force.

Irving, perhaps the greatest character actor of the century, was a special favourite with both the travelling public and railway employees. He was generous with his tips, friendly and nearly always approachable, unlike many other people in the news.

Locked gates in Station Street, during the railway strike 1911.

Birmingham Central Library.

During the 1890s, Saturday nights were frequently marred by young bloods of the city who, turned out of the local public houses, could buy extra drinks in the station refreshment rooms until 11.30 p.m. at the cost of a penny ticket, under the pretext of catching the last train to Harborne. The bar and refreshment room on platform one stayed open until the departure of the last train, but there were frequent fights and scuffles, several drunk and disorderly characters being taken in handcuffs to nearby Newton Street Police Station.

Birmingham race crowds were often difficult to handle and known at that period as 'the roughest of the rough'. At one time a gang of them, impatient of delay, were waiting for a train to Ayr Races and decided to raid the refreshment rooms on number three platform. Once inside they made insulting demands, clearing the bar-counter and shelves of everything to eat or drink within reach, but not offering to pay a penny-piece. Railway police were called in to restore order and one officer lost part of his ear in the ensuing free-for-all. Hostilities mainly consisted of kicking, biting — ear-lobes and noses being highly vulnerable — stamping or butting with the head. Offenders could only be detained in the station area for a short period and had to be charged at a city lock-up.

A few well-trained thieves operated from New Street, also card sharpers, some travelling in all parts of the country and almost living on the trains and in waiting rooms. They made rich hauls in empty compartments where items of luggage and personal belongings had been mislaid or forgotten. One afternoon a wealthy American, attending a Birmingham meeting of the Iron Master's Convention, had his dressing case placed on the seat of an empty compartment of a train waiting to leave platform one with a few minutes to spare, while he paced outside to finish his cigar. A railway policeman on the nearby footbridge chanced to see another man enter the compartment and drop the case out of the window on to the parallel tracks. The sneak-thief then jumped clear on the same side, recovered the case and scrambled on to platform two. Although managing to gain the steps and reach the exit the ruffian soon felt a hand on his collar and was taken to the detective's office, squirming and protesting. While waiting for the American to identify and claim his property, the thief stood in stolid silence, but seemed to be chewing something. A thump on the back and slight tap on the chin caused him to disgorge a mouthful of stolen pawn tickets. The American wished to drop the charge, as nothing was missing and the train could not be held longer. Yet he was forced to stay in Birmingham overnight, to appear at the Law Courts as an important witness.

A pickpocket taken to the detective's office noticed that a sash window had been left open, it being a hot day. While being questioned the man, well-past his better years, took a flying leap, but merely landed in the arms of another policeman, patrolling only a few yards away. He was returned to justice almost before his feet touched the ground.

In the *Birmingham Gazette* for the 14th August 1926 there was a short article devoted to the career of a Mr F. Stent, retired after fifty two years service at New Street Station. Mr Stent had joined the L.N.W.R. as a parcels boy in 1875 and served under seven District Superintendents. According to his remarks, when interviewed by the press: The footbridge at New Street was originally much narrower but higher. Luggage was man-handled across the tracks at great risk to the porters, as there were no subways or other crossings. The Central or Queen's Drive was not completed until 1885, much of it being the site of an old churchyard, great care and trouble being taken over the reinterment of the dead.

About a month later, in September 1926, *The Birmingham Post* recorded the memories of an Inspector Bevis, who had served on the railways for fifty years and had been at New Street for forty six of them. He commented that although during one period New Street claimed to be the largest station in the world the main part of the traffic was for local services. Many long distance trains skirted the centre of Birmingham, although stopping at Saltley in the north eastern suburbs, where they were met at an island platform by local connections from New Street, mainly short push-and-pull sets. Traffic to Scotland was negligible for many years and it was not until the cutting of the West Tunnel and other improvements of the late 1880s that long distance services began to boom, followed by a great expansion of all traffic.

Midland Railway Signal Cabin No. 2 on platform 5, south end.

Birmingham Central Library.

It was the opinion of Inspector Bevis that manners and behaviour were at a low ebb towards the end of the 19th century. In more recent years there had developed a higher sense of individual responsibility, with greater respect for property, both public and private. This attitude appears to have reached its peak shortly after the Second World War, although it would be interesting to make comparisons between the Victorian vandals and their great grandchildren of the 1980s! Due to the earlier closing of modern public houses there was less late travelling in the 1920s than before the First World War. On the whole crowds were much more orderly and subdued than when Queen Victoria graced the throne. Even those waiting for football specials and race trains during the 1920s gave very little trouble, while sorting out disorderly conduct on earlier race trains required courage and tact of the highest order.

Mr Bevis had worked as a porter, emergency guard, relief foreman and in many other grades, before becoming an inspector. He had often been a guard on the special trains used by Joseph Chamberlain during his political campaigns, at both local and national levels, most of them starting at New Street. There had always been good tips for the driver and himself at the end of each journey, with a word or two of personal thanks. In the old days far more people made use of special trains, both for themselves and large or small groups in their care. Some were only a single coach and brakevan behind a powerful tender locomotive, frequently ordered at short notice. Ordering a special could be done by anyone strolling on to the platform and asking to see the station master or someone in charge, but in later years it was necessary to apply in writing some time in advance, making a long-winded application to Railway Traffic Control at Saltley.

Members of the aristocracy and persons of high standing, frequently paid a courtesy visit to the station master when passing through New Street. This was partly out of respect for the official in question, being one of the higher grade or 'top-hat' station masters (always wearing a silk hat and frock coat while on duty), and partly to check the official time, which was almost a ritual. Important messages that might change a distinguished passenger's time of arrival or direction of travel were also frequently telegraphed to the station master's office. At New Street the station master's official clock was renowned for good time-keeping and above dispute. It was one of the three famous clocks on the L.N.W.R., the others being in the Board Room at Euston and at Lime Street, Liverpool.

The first motor car or horseless carriage came to New Street in 1896. This was unloaded without ceremony on to the carriage landing, which formed an extension to number three platform at its southern end. Man-handled into the Queen's Drive, it refused to start and was pushed up the slope to New Street by a volunteer gang of porters and cabbies. Most of the cab drivers were highly contemptuous, though amused, and claimed that such contraptions would never 'catch-on'. In the long term they proved hopelessly wrong as numerous motor cabs and private cars were taking over from the hansoms and growlers in less than a full decade.

Ex LNWR No 5000 Princess
Beatrice, *arriving at platform 3,*
New Street, 1928.

Permission W A Camwell.

2.

The Early 1900s

It is generally considered that the railways of Britain enjoyed their greatest prosperity from the early 1900s to the late 1920s, especially for passenger traffic. Although private motoring was on the increase and had gained respectability after the lifting of certain traffic restrictions, motoring for the masses was not a reality or even a valid dream until the mid-1930s. The majority of people of all classes travelled by train. Even long distance services by motor coach and charabanc were merely gaining a toehold in the period between the world wars. As New Street was essentially a passenger station, this was also the period of its greatest activity.

Journeys were made for business and pleasure with large numbers of commuters among the office, shop and factory workers, who either crossed the city or poured into its centre from outlying districts, by train or tram. With increasing emancipation and a greater number of jobs for women, especially in the shops and offices of central Birmingham, more unescorted females were using the trains (as may be seen in photographs of the 1900s) compared with those taken as little as ten years earlier. There were circular, if not circuitous routes serving the suburbs, all penetrating to the city centre and many terminating at New Street. Certain local trains were known to the station staff as 'round the world' or 'world tours'.

The tangle of running lines round Birmingham was not perhaps as intricate as those girdling London or Manchester, but sufficient for its needs and to maintain the honour of a great railway centre with more trains and connections to more destinations, than any other station in Britain. Since the demise of Snow Hill on the Western Region or former G.W.R. system, a modernised and almost totally rebuilt New Street still upholds the challenge as Britain's busiest railway centre.

While prosperity increased for some, during the early part of the century, others were less fortunate and may even have experienced a lower standard of living. Railway workers, at one time near the head of the industrial league both for wages and prestige, were gradually loosing ground to many employed in less skilled or responsible job-sectors, with cuts and restrictions, not related to public demand. There were railway strikes in 1911 and 1913, serious in their way but not as disruptive to the nation at the post-war strike of 1919, which — although lasting only ten days, started a movement away from railway travel from which the major systems never recovered. There is a pathetic photograph of strikers and their families standing in front of the padlocked gates of the Station Street entrance during one of the earlier strikes. Police and military protection was given to certain deliveries and installations, but the official presence was not so widely felt as nearly six years later. Yet during the interval a number of things had changed, including public attitudes.

The general mood of the 1900s was one of supressed optimism for both passengers and operatives. Even the weather played its part with a succession of long hot summers that brought out the blazers and boaters; holiday excursions running to Blackpool, Rhyl, Morecambe and other centres — mainly on the bracing coastline of North Wales and the North West of England. By arrangement with other railways it was also possible to reach the English Channel coast, a favourite holiday express for the south east being known as 'The Sunny South'. Yet fun and frivolity were merely an outward appearance, as both world affairs and internal discontent, especially in industry, seethed as though under the lid of a covered pot.

The first and most devastating upheaval came in the summer of 1914 with the outbreak of the First World War, during the greater part of which the railways were brought under a form of nationalisation. Restrictions and austerities were the order of the day, with full emphasis placed on the movement of troops, hospital trains and other services vital to the war effort. This was a strange paradox as during the four months from early May to late August all records had been broken for excursion and holiday traffic on most of the main lines of Britain. As might be expected, large numbers of the travelling public, between late 1914 and 1918, were seen to be wearing uniform, encumbered by all types of awkward gear and equipment.

Sketch map of railway network in the centre of Birmingham during the 1920s and 1930s.

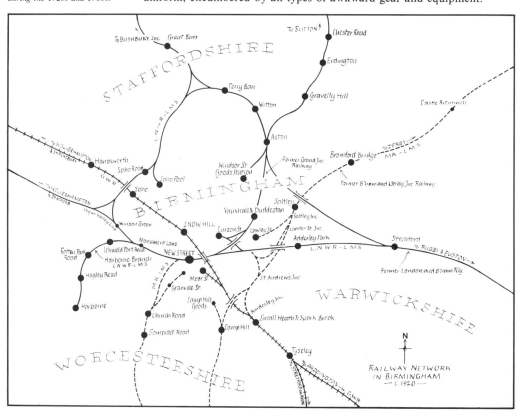

36

Platform 3, looking north, during the 1900s.

F Hubball Collection.

NEW STREET STATION, BIRMINGH

The First World War.

In New Street platforms were crowded with service personnel entraining for Flanders or even more far-flung places in three continents, until then virtually unknown. Grief-striken families clung to the tails of greatcoats while rifles, packs and water bottles were frequently mislaid, turning up in the least expected places. Troops from mounted units, of which there were still large numbers throughout the conflict, wore hooked steel spurs that were a great danger both to themselves and other passengers, especially when boarding in-coming trains. Men in unfamiliar hob-nailed boots, weighed down by their kit like pack mules, slithered dangerously near the platform edges.

On the public footbridge armed military police made spotchecks on servicemen, it being their duty to examine passes and catch deserters or those over-staying their leave.

From the 9th of August 1914, during the period of full-mobilisation all mainline stations in Birmingham were closed. In those days every regiment and corps had its compliment of horse transport, which had to accompany troop trains either to training areas or the front line. Horses were bluffed or coaxed into unfamiliar horse boxes or cattle trucks, from the loading docks in Station Street and the Queen's Drive, while a motley array of General Service wagons, limbers, travelling cookers and mess carts were sheeted-up and rolled on to carriage trucks. Troop movements by rail were then trumpcards in wartime strategy, especially before the 90 per cent mechanisation of modern armies.

Throughout the First World War, tens of thousands of guns, rifles and other arms were trans-shipped to the front line via New Street, Birmingham factories then being the hub of the national small arms industry.

By 1916 the daily number of trains using New Street was 700, with 20,000,000 passengers per annum.

The Railway Strike of 1919

A return to peacetime conditions was marred, less than twelve months after the Armistice, by the railway strike of 1919, which began on 26th September. According to newspaper headlines, 'Chaos Reigns at Birmingham Stations'. People stranded at New Street on the day the strike began were told that the 11.50 a.m. train would be the last to leave for northern cities. On platform three there was a near-riot involving angry passengers and railway staff, although members of the public were brought to their senses by an anonymous ex-drill sergeant booming out words of command that drew the throng first to attention and later into the safety of the Queen's Drive without further protest. So many people had been trained by the services in wartime that their reflexes were still almost totally conditioned by such domination. On this occasion a moment of prompt action saved several broken scalps and perhaps more serious injuries.

It was later announced that a train would leave for Rugby at 2 p.m. but this had to be cancelled as the guard was a Birmingham man and could not be guaranteed a safe return journey. The driver and fireman were both from Rugby, as eager to beat the travel ban as their passengers. Yet without a guard no-one could travel in safety, to the great disgust of those already boarding the empty carriages. On the stroke of two, however, the train was abandoned with a great slamming of doors. Within minutes every platform was deserted, apart from a small handful of officials, stray pigeons and the station cats. The gates were locked and police ordered to watch the exits while awaiting the arrival of armed troops. These eventually came in army lorries, with fixed bayonets and steelhelmets, although even greater fuss seems to have been made at Snow Hill than at New Street. Snow Hill, on the Great Western system, was to become the temporary headquarters of the Worcestershire Regiment, there being ample facilities for camping-out in the large covered concourse opening off Livery Street.

On the 30th September more troops were brought in, with two battalions of the King's Royal Rifles driven into the loading bay off Station Street or deposited in Stephenson Place. Like the Worcesters before them, they were wearing full kit and those appearing in Station Street were roundly cheered by passers-by, many of whom lingered to form the nucleus of a crowd. Yet before long the gates clanged shut a second time, sentries were mounted and patrols organised . . . civilian police requesting the public to 'move on in an orderly manner."

At the time of the strike there were numerous horses from the shunting and cartage departments, stabled on railway property, many under the arches of viaducts. There were also cattle and other livestock in transit, all of which had to be fed and watered at regular intervals. Railwaymen normally in charge of these duties volunteered to run an emergency service, as they had done in pre-war strikes on both the railways and the canals, but in 1919 a tougher line was taken and they were dissuaded from such humane actions by the intervention of union officials. Rescue work had to be organised through the good offices of the R.S.P.C.A. and other animal charities. There were then over 14,000 men and 1,000 horses based on the Birmingham depots.

The strike was over on the morning of the 7th October, but side effects were further reaching. Despite appeals in the newspapers and at public meetings, numerous essential journeys had to be made and enterprising businessmen from large concerns to small or individual operators were soon cashing-in on a public need. The 'Midland Red' bus service ran its first regular trips to London, while car-owners offered to take three or four passengers to London, in a single direction, at £2 per head, at their own risk.

There was also flying in antique biplanes from Castle Bromwich Aerodrome, which lay to the north east of Birmingham. People were taken to the flying field in a fleet of cars and taxis, being charged £15 for a journey starting in Stephenson Place and ending at Hendon airport. There were normally four persons per cabin plane, but some were strapped into open cockpits, having to wear elaborate regulation flying gear.

Unfortunately for the railways, people came to enjoy flying and accustomed to road transport, while long distance buses and motor coaches were even cheaper than trains, if slower in those days and less reliable. Many regular travellers did not look back, alternative forms of transport had made a successful challenge and the slow but certain decline of railway passenger services had begun. There was a further strike in 1924 but with limited services and special trains for coal, meat and perishables. During the general strike of 1926 trains were frequently manned and operated by outside volunteers, with past railway experience, often under police or military guard.

The Station Street entrance, New Street, 1959.

The railways attempted to counter their loss of revenue with cheap day and half-day trips to London and other important centres. A day trip to Euston cost as little as 6s (old money). Trips to Manchester, Stockport and Sheffield, at the same period, were a shilling cheaper. Bank Holiday excursions to Douglas, in the Isle of Man, were advertised in the Birmingham Mail as 26s 6d (old money). Yet it was not until the Easter period of 1922 that holiday traffic and cheap excursions returned to pre-war normality.

One of the benefits of rail travel was the chance to buy a cheap but nourishing meal, either on the trains (as a time-saver) or in refreshment rooms and restaurants, then conveniently sited in most stations. A few shillings, seldom more than half a crown ($12\frac{1}{2}$p.), would purchase a three-course meal, brought to the table by polite and dexterous waiters whose skill with plates of hot soup in the gangways of speeding trains was worthy of a circus act.

The Midland side from Station Street, at the junction with Hill Street. Ridge and furrow roofs in foreground protect the fish dock and back sidings. Early 1920s.

Birmingham Central Library.

40

Tragic Interlude

There was an unfortunate accident on the 27th November 1921, in the Midland part of the station, this being one of the most serious disasters recorded at New Street. Three deaths and fourteen injuries were reported, although only one man was detained in hospital — suffering from a fractured spine, from which he recovered.

The persons killed were a man named Willson of Tamworth, aged 43, leaving a wife and three children; also a single man named Cosgrave, aged 35, living in Handsworth, Birmingham. A third victim was the infant daughter of a soldier named Dunkerley stationed in Ireland.

It was stated that "the 4.12 for Tamworth, delayed by engine trouble, was still standing alongside number four platform with its rear coaches opposite the bookstall by the bridge, when the express from Cheltenham and Bristol, due at 4.27 a.m., ran into the station prompt on time. The signals were stated to have been against the train and circumstances of the accident were to be the subject of a Government Enquiry." A preliminary hearing was to be held by the railway company on the morning of the 29th November, while an inquest was ordered for the same afternoon.

At the time of the crash "passengers and officials realised the danger as the express swept round the long curve approaching the platform and, in response to their cries, a number jumped from the stationery train a second or two before impact. Ticket-inspector Barrington, near the tail of the Tamworth train, was instrumental in saving several persons from death and injury, shouting warnings through the windows of the rear compartments when he could well have run to safety. The powerful express engine struck the rear guardsvan of the Tamworth train as people were still trying to get out. The guardsvan seems to have broken away from its bogies but rammed into the nearest passenger coach, and the top structure of this also became free. The two vehicle bodies rose together at a sharp angle or diagonal, and there was a grave danger of further telescoping or severe blows prior to a piling-up movement. This, however, was prevented by the roof of the passenger coach at the fore-end engaging and coming to rest on a ledge of the footbridge, where the two structures were interlocked."

Frank Arthur Fisher, a parcels foreman had a narrow escape. At the moment of impact he was in the guardsvan glancing at the headlines of a newspaper. He was flung on his back and, as the van rose in the air, he rolled to one side on top of some mailbags which cushioned his fall. He received neither scratch nor bruise and later assisted in salvage and rescue work.

Debris had to be loaded on to several trucks run alongside, and it was impossible to use either number four or five up lines for several hours, all trains having to work from other platforms, while a number of local services were suspended for the day. A full hearing was adjourned to the 20th December, but the company agreed to accept full responsibility and meet all reasonable claims for damages.

The Official Enquiry was held under the auspices of Colonel Pringle, acting on behalf of the Ministry of Transport. Numerous witnesses were drawn from railway staff and passengers assembled on platform four at the time of the disaster.

41

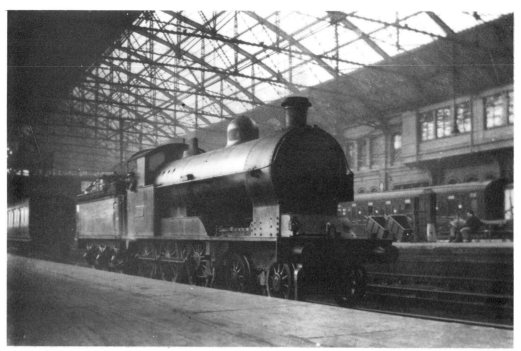

A ticket collector who saw the express approach stated that he thought, "the brakes had not been applied; if they had the smash would not have happened."

The guard of the express said, "the brakes were applied all the way through the tunnel and he did not notice they had been released."

The driver, after stating that he had over twenty years experience of working trains into New Street, and that on the day of the accident his brakes were in good order, elected to give the remainder of his evidence in private. The same course was also taken by his fireman, which concluded the first stage of the enquiry.

At a later session the exemption from block signalling, of the platform road, was called into question. Exemption for this had been granted by the Board of Trade at an earlier period, and applied to operations between No 5 Box and No 1 Box, also between No 5 Box and No 2 Box. Traffic was controlled only by stop signals on the platforms, a system which had operated for thirty years without accident or complaint. In further evidence it was claimed that the absolute block system was not practicable in large stations such as New Street. At the time of the crash there had been misty conditions in the station with vision obscured and moist rails on which the wheels skidded. The train was proved to have over-run the signals and the driver admitted to a fatal error. To further confuse matters he appears to have misheard his fireman to say the signal was 'off' when it was 'on'. When applying the brakes the wheels slipped and the engine was virtually out of control. There was a verdict of accidental death, with no criminal implications.

Only nine months after the crash on platform four there was almost a carbon copy of the previous accident, but without serious injuries. According to the *Birmingham Gazette* for the 5th August 1922 the 4.40 p.m. train from Brighton and the south ran into the rear of empty coach-stock of a local train, standing opposite number two platform. There were no deaths and only minor cuts and bruises to report, even the locomotive being able to move away under its own steam. The driver in charge was a passed-fireman who had not previously driven a passenger train. Failure to see or understand the signals did not arise and the accident was blamed solely on excessive speed, not allowing enough time to pull-up. It was noted that the entrance to New Street Station was among the most difficult sections of the road in this area. At a subsequent enquiry it was recommended that all firemen in charge of passenger trains should submit to more searching practical examinations. Derailment of stock required the services of a breakdown crane, with diversions lasting several hours.

The first all-steel carriages and trains were announced in 1926, made locally at the Birmingham Carriage and Wagon Works. These were planned to be much safer in time of collision, almost fireproof and unlikely to collapse or splinter on impact.

Returning to Normal

In the *Birmingham Gazette* for the 12th March 1922 there was a short article on the reintroduction of pre-war summer fares and a resumption of

Ex LNWR Locomotive No 1772 backing on to a train platform 3. 1926.

Photo: J T Clewley Permission W A Camwell.

Ex LNWR saddle tank No 3615 shunting ex Great Eastern Railway coaching stock on middle road between platforms 2 and 3. New Street, 1926.

Photo: J T Clewley Permission W A Camwell.

excursions to leading resorts, also to important towns and cities throughout the British Isles. Holiday travel was to be based on single fares and a third, for double journeys, with single fares for day excursions. On Good Friday and Easter Monday there would be Midland Railway excursions to Burton, Derby, Matlock Bath, Darley Dale, Rowsley, Bakewell and Worcester, while on Easter Monday only there were fast through-trains to Cheltenham Spa, Gloucester, Bristol, Weston-Super-Mare, Chesterfield, Sheffield, Rotherham, Leeds and Bradford. Cheap day and half-day excursions were also to be run to Nuneaton, Hinckley, Leicester and other centres in the East Midlands.

The London and North Western offered attractive day trips to Rhyl, Colwyn Bay, Llandudno, Blackpool, Fleetwood, Southport, Lancaster and and Morecambe on Thursday and Saturday. There were also trips to Scotland and Ireland, over the Easter period, at less than half price.

The Grouping

In 1923 the London and North Western Railway Company, having previously absorbed the Lancashire and Yorkshire Railway (1922), was amalgamated with the Midland Railway and other groups to form the London, Midland and Scottish Railway. The Scottish part of the company was mainly represented — north of the border — by the Caledonian Railway and lesser undertakings associated with the West Highlands and west coast

Waiting for an excursion. Taken during the 1950s, this scene was typical of many such at New Street during the preceeding fifty years.

Birmingham Post & Mail.

44

routes. These arrangements had been made as part of the official railway groupings of 1922/23, in a belated attempt to rationalise an unwieldly system that seemed to benefit, during the First World War, from greater unity of control. By this measure over four hundred companies were reduced to four. Yet while there may have been too many small independent groups, some unworkable in modern practice, difficulties that might be overcome in a crisis were not always solvable in normal conditions.

There may have been less strife between the remaining main line companies, as a result of amalgamations, but even more rivalry within each group, arising from competition rather than co-operation, often tinged with more than a hint of jealousy. The L.N.W.R., as the Premier Line, expected to remain a single unit to which others were merely added, as appeared to be the case with the Great Western Railway (the only pre-grouping company to retain its original identity). Instead the Midland Railway seemed to dominate the partnership, although problems arising were perhaps less acute at New Street than in other places as both constituents in Birmingham had already worked together for about seventy years. At the time of amalgamation it may be noted that the Midland had the highest portion of share capital which was £205,000,000, against the London and North Western's £132,000,000 — although the contribution of the Lancashire and Yorkshire was a further £73,000,000.

There were eventually four divisions of the L.M.S. for locomotive workings and general operations, New Street being in the centre of the Midland or First Division. It was also covered by the Western or 'A' Division of the former L.N.W.R. routes. Engine numbering was 1 to 4,999 (Midland) and 10,000 to 13,999 (Western). London, Midland and Scottish liveries were maroon and black for locomotives and coaching stock, the maroon almost identical with, but sometimes a shade darker, than Midland Railway lake. Midland passenger locomotives had been crimson lake, lined-out in black and yellow, although in the early days locomotives had appeared in mid-green liveries. Eventually all Midland goods engines were black, which later applied to L.M.S. motive power in this category. Carriages of the Midland were crimson lake with lining-out in straw-yellow.

There were few named locomotives on the Midland Railway at any period. L.N.W.R. livery was blue-black lined with red, having blocked yellow lining on the cab side sheets of all locomotives. Carriages were an unusual shade of purple-brown to the waistline with eggshell white above, looking black and white in the distance or when the stock needed repainting. Many L.N.W.R. locomotives had exotic names such as *'Luck of Edenhall'* (frequently seen at New Street), *Queen of the Belgians* and *Merry Carlisle*. It took a number of years to repaint the existing locomotives and rolling stock in their new colours. Some of the L.N.W.R. types appeared much neglected, their dark liveries obscured by layers of dirt and grime until withdrawn.

As a development arising from the grouping, a new range of locomotives was introduced while others were given a chance to show their paces on unfamiliar metals. This did not affect the routes through New Street as much as other branches of the same system, especially as major contacts between London and the north were increasingly bypassed by the Trent Valley line from Rugby to Stafford. With trains to and from Birmingham it was, in many cases, 'the mixture as before'. As an exception Standard Midland Compounds from the old Midland Railway, were frequently switched to ex-L.N.W.R. metals, helping to run two-hourly services between New Street and Euston, revived after the war and operated as a prestige effort to challenge similar runs by the G.W.R. from Snow Hill.

The 4-4-0 'Crimson Ramblers' were eventually more at home on the south eastern route out of Birmingham than travelling in a north easterly direction towards their home centre of Derby. They seldom worked south west to Bristol until a much later period, as this part of the route was usually dominated by shorter and lighter passenger trains. From personal recollections, however, most of the passenger trains working through to New Street — during the late 1930s, over the high level lines at Tamworth, were Midland compounds, not infrequently doubleheaded. Like many locomotives with 4-4-0 wheel arrangements, the 'compounds' tended to sway or hunt, especially at speed. They were not at first liked by former L.N.W.R. crews, partly because they could not be flogged and as a matter of simple prejudice, their introduction on certain routes almost leading to strike action.

The Two-Hour Expresses

Rivalry, as previously mentioned, between the L.N.W.R. and the G.W.R.,

Ex LNWR 2-4-2ST No 6542 standing in the South Staffordshire bay on platform 1. 1927.

Photo: J T Clewley Permission W A Camwell.

Ex North Staffordshire Railway locomotive at New Street, later absorbed into LMS stock. 1926.

Photo: J T Clewley Permission W A Camwell.

for the fastest timings between London and Birmingham, led to great improvements in the services offered by both companies. The race commenced in 1852 and continued with certain breaks until the period between the world wars. The best L.N.W.R. run of 1902 was two hours five minutes. This was improved to two hours and a regular two-hourly service left New Street each weekday, as from the 1st March 1905. The G.W.R. had a clear advantage from July 1910, when they opened a new line in South Warwickshire, known as the Aynho Cut-off, which reduced their run by several miles. Honours were, at this point, evenly divided within the limits of sense and safety.

To make their services more attractive to businessmen the L.N.W.R. introduced a secretarial service of expert stenographers, able to type on portable machines while bowling along at a mile a minute. The girls in question were plainly but attractively dressed, although discouraged from the over-use of scents and cosmetics. They mainly appeared on the early morning and evening expresses that terminated at Wolverhampton High Level.

The two hour speed record was first broken on the 30th September 1935, when an L.M.S. passenger express left Euston at 9.15 a.m. and arrived in New Street Station at nine and a half minutes past eleven. It was scheduled to

The footbridge during the early 1930s.

48

reach Birmingham at 11.10 and the fact that it was half a minute ahead of time showed that there had been no great strain on men or machinery. The train was drawn by one of the new 'Silver Jubilee' engines of the L.M.S. The driver was Joseph Cox of Bushbury with 41 years railway service to his credit, while the fireman was W. Reynolds of Wolverhampton. Both men were said to have worn smiles of satisfaction as they were congratulated by Mr Joseph Harrison, the station master at New Street. Only one halt had been made — at Willesden Junction — from which the non-stop run was made in $103^1/_2$ minutes, the distance being $107^1/_2$ miles. The highest speeds were 77 m.p.h. near Bletchley and 75 m.p.h. between Coventry and Birmingham.

Time allowed from Euston was 1 hour 55 minutes and the train arrived $^1/_2$ minute ahead of schedule, despite the fact that speed had to be cut to 30 m.p.h. through Brandon, near Rugby, due to colliery subsidence. Even greater speeds could have been attained, but it was the practice of the company to keep something in hand as a reserve for contingencies. The record breaking train had 11 coaches, weighing, with passengers and luggage, about 355 tons.

It was further announced that on the same evening the L.M.S. would bring into operation a new record-schedule for the fastest train on its own system. "This will be the 6.20 p.m. from New Street to Euston, which will be accelerated to run to Watford, a distance of 65 miles, at an average speed — start to stop — of over 60 m.p.h."

Reconstruction Plans

Early in 1923 plans were discussed to build either a further footbridge across New Street Station or a vehicular bridge 60ft wide, running from Stephenson Place to John Bright Street, at a high level. The idea of a second footbridge had been discussed in 1913/14 but shelved due to the outbreak of the First World War. Such work was partly to fulfil a genuine need for expansion but also intended to find relief for the local unemployed and demobilised ex-servicemen. Half the total costs were to be met by the railways and half by the Public Works Department.

Regarding the existing footbridge, despite the unwritten rule to keep left, both on bridge and steps, there were frequent delays and confusions among pedestrians, especially between 8.30 and 9.30 in the mornings, at lunch time and between 4.30 and 6.30 in the early evenings.

A year later there were suggestions, if not actual plans and proposals, to abolish the Queen's Drive and remove the carriage landings, while joining-up the bays, in order to make room for more running lines and passenger platforms. There were even new designs for the station as a whole, especially in 1932 and 1936. These were to have been futuristic buildings with several layers or levels, having not only platforms for main line trains but an underground station for local services, a coach or bus station, a sports stadium — with provision for ice-hockey and boxing, and an air strip for helicopter landings. Yet although elaborate drawings, artist's impressions and scale models were produced this was the era of depression and funds were no longer available for large-scale works of this type. It may be noted that the 1936 proposals were submitted by two young Canadian engineers visiting Birmingham.

49

3

Between the Wars

Mr J. Harrison, the station master at New Street, gave an interesting lecture to the local 'Historical and Philosophical Society', in May 1935, on the work of his station.

He mentioned that, by the mid-1930s, passenger traffic comprised 25,000,000 people per annum, with 3,000 trains per week. During the normal rush hours, trains arrived and departed at approximately $1^1/_2$ minute intervals. In a recent analysis of local trains on the Western Division side of New Street, it was proved that out of a total of 3,261 some 2,444 trains were "on time exactly", while 662 were one to five minutes late. There was an operating staff of 500.

New Street was a national traffic filter "through which most trains, including specials for shows or sporting events and parcels traffic, must pass as quickly and safely as possible. Delays and accidents would otherwise cause disorganisation not only in Birmingham but over large areas of the whole system. There were by 1935, 14 platforms, eight for through running, with six bays and six signal boxes. A large part of the parcels traffic ran at night."

It was recorded that 30,000,000 parcels and packages were forwarded annually, while 13,000 tons of fish were delivered to the back sidings or fish dock, mainly from Yarmouth and Grimsby. Although horses were gradually being replaced by mechanical transport, at least 1,000 came to New Street each year, in the delivery service alone.

Other traffic, not classed as parcels, could be anything from 2 cwts. upwards. This included fresh fruit, cut flowers, meat, cakes,machinery and machinery parts, amounting to 5,000 tons per annum. There was also an important cycle traffic with 48,000 pedal cycles and 8,000 motor cycles despatched from New Street each year. The cycle traffic mainly operated from platforms one and six, especially the latter.

A General Description of New Street in the 1920s and 1930s

Entering the station from Stephenson Place the would-be passenger found himself in the main booking hall and passenger concourse. The public footbridge was reached after descending a flight of stairs with a centre-handrail, governed by an unofficial 'keep left' rule. On the bridge were two shops, with a bookstall at the Station Street end and numerous large show cases. The latter were almost like shop windows, frequently illuminated day and night displaying the goods of both city stores and the gadgets and small machine parts of local manufacturers. In one show case there was even a full-sized motor cycle. Further steps, again with centre-handrails, led down to each platform, on opposite sides of the footbridge. Harborne branch trains nearly always left from the bay siding near the wall, at the northern end of platform one. Local Stour Valley trains used the parallel line in the same bay.

Signalbox No 4, on platform 5. Loading mailbags on a local train.

Brian Timmins.

51

Stock was usually backed-in by a station pilot from Monument Lane Shed. On this side of the station supplies were brought in for sleeping cars and restaurant cars, either from the Queen's Hotel or other storage space, on that side of the building. Bays at the other end of the platform were used by trains to Aston, Walsall and Lichfield.

Most of the London traffic left from number one platform, including the two-hour expresses. This was also the arrival platform from the north west and for long distance trains approaching over the Stour Valley line. Trains in a southerly direction were handled by Midland 'Compounds', 'Patriots' and later Stanier designed locomotives from Bushbury. At an earlier period there would be a wide selection of 'Bloomers', 'Precursors', 'Jumbo ' 'Precedents', 'Prince of Wales' and 'George Fifth'-type engines.

All platforms were served by a middle road for stabling parcel vans and other spare items of stock. Considerable inwards traffic on this side of the station also worked into number two platform, which was an island divided into sections A and B. There were no buildings of any type on this platform. Each platform had signboards with direction fingers showing when and where the next train would arrive or leave, several surmounted by a clock face or dial giving the schedules. Some of the platforms were not quite long enough for their purpose, especially in dealing with long distance expresses. This meant a certain amount of drawing-up, regulated by dwarf signals, some on the footbridge and others at a much lower level, controlled by pointsmen or from the open box on the bridge. There were no movements from any platform until the 'all-clear' had been given by platform inspectors. Due to lack of block workings in the station area there was always close consultation between platform staff, inspectors and signalmen. When it was time for a train to leave a bell would be rung, operated by a press-button at the end of each platform. This cleared the signalman who in turn cleared the guard. A wave of the hand above the head meant that all doors must be closed, followed by a wave of the green flag or lamp to warn the footplate crew.

Trains out of New Street were only allowed one pilot, although two were frequently allowed at Euston and some other large stations. Only trains with fifteen fewer bogies were allowed into or out of New Street.

Traffic from platform three worked in a north westerly direction with main line arrivals from London and the south. A considerable parcels traffic was prepared on this side with vans marshalled on the middle road for Crewe and points north. The carriage landing on the L.N.W.R. side was at the southern end of platform three. A bay at the nothern end was known as the Coffeehouse Siding, backing on to a former refreshment room of that name.

Beyond the central carriageway or Queen's Drive was the Midland part of the station, handling arrivals and departures for Leeds, York, Sheffield, Bristol, Gloucester and suburban trains on the former Midland branches, also services to the Eastern counties and East Midlands. Several of the buildings on this side were of slatted wooden construction. Platform five was mainly concerned with holiday excursions and traffic to Leicester or destinations in East Anglia, including Yarmouth and Norwich. Trains halted by bridge signals on platforms four and five — also on platform two, had to stand well-clear of the cross-over roads. Platform six was the most widely

used on the Midland side, having the main offices for this part of the station, including a large refreshment room and restaurant. All traffic was banked-out from this platform, to Church Road Junction, the banker usually kept in number six bay. Many trains on this route were also double-headed. There would be numerous wicker baskets on platform six containing hotel linen and other stores, returned as empties from platform four. Sleeping car linen was laundered at Vauxhall. New crockery for the refreshment rooms was supplied from St. Helens, Lancashire.

The fish dock and carriage landing were to the rear of platform six, at the north end, while there was a platform for handling parcels traffic at the southern end. There were refreshment rooms or buffets on all platforms except number two platform, although the refreshment room on platform four eventually became a staff canteen.

There were no special mail trains but post office vans were attached to certain expresses or fast passenger trains, usually at the front or locomotive end. The 9.55 p.m. from number four platform took most of the mails to the north east. Considerable mail traffic was also tranferred to the Trent Valley line at Tamworth, taken from high to low level stations.

The overnight sleeper from Glasgow terminated at New Street, about 5.50 a.m. each weekday morning. Those occupying a sleeping car berth were warned in advance and given half an hour to vacate their compartment. After unloading the sleeping cars were run down to Vauxhall, where beds would be stripped and changed by a squad of 'fresh linen women'.

Other important trains were the 3 a.m. 'Rabbit Train' from Yeovil (which brought not only a supply of rabbits for the Birmingham markets but also quantities of dairy produce from the south west), and the so-called 'Newsman' from Euston. The latter started from London with about fifteen vans of newspapers, journals and magazines. It was frequently headed by a 'Precursor'-type locomotive but sometimes by an 'Experiment'. About eight vans were dropped-off at Rugby with a van for Coventry, five for New Street and a further single forwarded to Wolverhampton. At New Street papers were collected by road vehicles on number three platform, in the Queen's Drive.

All long distance trains arriving in New Street were inspected by wheel tappers and examiners from the carriage and wagon department, who not only tapped wheels but examined springs and couplings, chalking their comments—with dates and times—on the underframes.

All platforms were connected by subways to deal with mail, luggage and parcels traffic. From the 1930s the 4ft long hand-trollies were mainly towed by petrol tractors, some trollies and barrows raised to platform level in special lifts worked by hydraulic power or water motors. Special trollies brought mail bags from the Post Office in Hill Street, in long trains, each trolley piled to an incredible height. G.P.O. tractor-units were powered by electricity rather than petrol. The G.P.O. drivers rode on the front of their vehicles and were extremely skilful at weaving round items of luggage or groups of people, without accidents. Parcel porters designated to assist the G.P.O. staff in clearing the mails, were in a different grade to ordinary parcel porters.

Water for use in lavatories and kitchen cars was brought on to platforms one and three in special water-barrel carts. Supplies were fed through apertures in the roof by means of piping, the tanks filled by hand pumping, a manual operation throughout. While this was being done there was usually someone on the roof and the carriage to be serviced would have a warning flag attached. A similar type of two-wheeled vehicle was also used to supply gas, in the days before electric lighting. Pilot lights could be pushed on by prodding with rods from the underside of the carriages.

Tea Trollies

These paraded up and down the main platforms, at least until the wartime period, offering a selection of wrapped sandwiches and slab cake. There was a large vertical tea urn at one end of the trolley, presided over by a girl dressed as a waitress with starched cap and apron. This service was controlled by the Queen's Hotel.

Theatrical Traffic

Until the mid-1950s there had always been a fair number of theatres and music halls in Birmingham. Even after the Second World War touring companies and shows frequently visited the area as part of their nation-wide circuit, at least before television and bingo began to kill-off this type of live entertainment. Such companies moved about with their own scenery and props, which were sent by rail in specially designed items of rolling stock known as scenery vans. These latter had end loading and roofs arched fairly high under the loading gauge. Most larger shows needed at least two vans with sometimes an extra van for special effects. They would be backed into sidings on the Station Street side of New Street nearly every Saturday evening, loading any time after the last house, between 11 p.m. and early Sunday morning. Most of the costumes would be brought from the stage door in wicker-baskets under the supervision of the wardrobe mistress.

Once the vans were ready two or three passenger coaches would be added for the cast, under-studies, scene painters and technicians, although stars might prefer to travel by ordinary trains or had their own transport. The theatre train finally left Birmingham any time after two o'clock on Sunday morning picking up its passengers on number three platform, but sometimes on the Midland side, when the show was to visit Sheffield or Leeds. When the time for departure was settled a locomotive would be sent down from Monument Lane.

General Operations

Operations at New Street were of a fairly consistent and unchanging pattern, throughout the life of the old station, at least from the 1890s. They altered very little after the 1923 grouping, until after the Second World War.

On the L.N.W.R. side trains ran between Euston and Birmingham, some terminating at Wolverhampton High Level. There were also long distance trains to and from North Wales, Liverpool, Manchester, Carlisle and Glasgow, via Stafford, Crewe and Wolverhampton. Some trains to Manchester, however, took an alternative route via Stoke and Macclesfield. On the Midland side the main services were between York or Leeds and Sheffield to the north east, and to Bristol in the south west, via Derby,

Cheltenham and Gloucester—with Birmingham south of centre on this route. Tamworth was reached on the Derby line via its High Level Station. Semi-fast routes were a direct link with the East Midlands and Eastern counties, sometimes with foreign engines and stock from other systems or regions. Shortly after the Second World War the Eastern Region BI 4-6-0 tender engines were fairly common on the Midland side usually heading trains for Peterborough, Cambridge, Yarmouth or Norwich. Trains for the east passed through or connected with Leicester, Nuneaton, Hinckley and Melton Mowbray.

Local trains on L.N.W.R. metals reached Harborne, the Perry Barr circular route, Sutton Coldfield, Lichfield and Burton-on-Trent. Other trains ran to Coventry, Kenilworth and Leamington, or to Wolverhampton High Level via Dudley Port. Many of the smaller trains were handled by tank engines and 0-6-2 coal tanks were very much in evidence up to the time of nationalisation.

Midland locals also covered a circular route, this being to New Street and back via the Lifford Curve, Hazelwell and Camp Hill. The latter service tended to bypass Kings Norton. Other trains using part of this line worked to Redditch (which had a small sub-shed connected to Bournville), Ashchurch and Evesham. Midland stopping trains also served Walsall (South Staffordshire route) via the Aldridge, Sutton Park line, further running to Wolverhampton High Level via Short Heath, with branch connections to Brown Hills. Stopping trains ran to Burton-on-Trent and Derby with numerous halts, including Saltley, Castle Bromwich, Water Orton, Kingsbury, Wilnecote and Tamworth High Level.

Signal Boxes

Until the rebuilding programme of the 1960s New Street was controlled by six main signal boxes.

Train movements to and from the platforms for London, and both up and down lines at the London end, were controlled by two men in number one box, with sixty three levers. This was at the southern throat of the station near the archway for the Worcester Street Bridge, separated from a stable used by shunting horses — partly under the bridge — by a dead-end siding.

Number two box was controlled by one signalman with seventy five levers, mainly reponsible for Midland Division lines at the south end. It was situated on the platform, near the end-ramp, on platform number five.

Number three box or cabin shared the duties of number one box, also the control of certain dwarf signals at platform level and on the footbridge. It was demolished, with the overall roof and other features on this side of the station, shortly after the Second World War. It was single manned.

Number four box, with seventy three levers, was also single manned. It controlled both running lines and the back sidings with traffic to platforms seven, eight, nine, ten and eleven. This was also on platform five but at the Gloucester end.

The largest signal box in the station was number five, having one hundred and fifty three levers, operated by three men. It controlled all traffic, platforms and sidings at the Stour Valley or Wolverhampton approaches. It occupied an island site, between running lines, on the far side of the Hill Street bridge.

Looking towards the back sidings from platform 4.

Brian Timmins.

57

Number six box was a small structure at track level, partly concealed by the Navigation Street bridge. It had an eighteen level frame and was operated by a single man. It controlled movements at the end of number one platform and cross-over points leading into the Stour Valley bays.

Many of the former L.N.W.R. signals were retained in the style later adopted by the L.M.S., although replaced by upper quadrant types from the 1930s. Midland Railway signal posts, many long enduring, were noted for highly decorative, spiked-finials.

A major signalling change came to New Street in 1924, when colour light signals or 'robots' replaced lower quadrant types (mechanical stop signals) on platforms seven and eight. Colour light signals were also fixed to the over-bridge in place of semaphores, in 1946. Other colour light signals were introduced on the Midland side in 1952. A system of track circuiting was introduced between 1942 and 1946.

Uniforms

Platform staff wore drab uniforms of dark blue, almost black, serge. They were issued with peaked caps having L.M.S. on a wide cotton band above the peak. A further band, about half an inch in width, fitted with small buckles, could be adjusted as a chin strap for blustery weather, but was seldom worn in this way. The initials of the railway company were also worked on jacket lapels in coloured threads. Buttons were of chromium or bright metal and had to be kept shining and untarnished, not the easiest of tasks in a polluted atmosphere.

Platform inspectors and foremen wore a uniform of slightly better cut and quality, in a lighter shade of blue. Passenger guards wore silver braid and piping. During the late 1920s, after the grouping, the uniforms of inspectors and guards greatly improved, both in style and quality, but those of porters did not change much. Signalmen wore much the same type of uniform as porters, including a sleeved waistcoat. In the early days guards on goods trains, wore nothing to show their grade, even when they sometimes worked passenger trains. They were later upgraded to the use of silver braid while guards on long distance passenger trains and expresses were promoted to gold braid and gilt buttons, with gold piping on cap and jacket.

The smartest uniforms were worn by the staff of the Queen's Hotel, especially the commissionaires and doormen. Hotel porters patrolled the bridge and frequently met long distance trains, wearing smart red jackets, their caps stiffened by wires in the seams. Most waiters wore full evening dress while those in the refreshment rooms on the platforms wore ankle-length aprons.

Cartage Department uniforms for draymen were similar to those for platform staff, although some wore short aprons. The parcel van drivers or carmen, also the drivers of motor vehicles, wore smartly cut riding breeches and leggings.

Some of the dirtiest jobs in the station were performed by the passenger or coach shunters, who must have needed a change of uniform every day. They frequently crawled under or between the carriages at rail level, handling pipes and connections that were caked in mud or grease.

There were numerous outside porters, not wearing official uniforms, apart from a peaked cap and arm-band. The band was worn on the left arm above the elbow, having a numbered brass plate, with the words Outside Porter in raised letters. These men may have been pensioners or part-time workers, employed in a number of odd jobs. Many of them pushed small hand-barrows from the back sidings, up to the Market Hall, loaded with crates of fish and vegetables. Shop keepers from local towns such as Walsall, Dudley and Tamworth frequently ordered fish, fruit and vegetables from the market and would tip the outside men to wheel these back to the station on their return trips, to be placed in the care of a guard on the next local train.

Signs and Advertisements.

An interesting feature of New Street station was the variety of advertising and its numerous enamelled signs, many of which were made by firms based either in Birmingham or the nearby Black Country. These were to be found from the 1880s, on all retaining and curtain walls, the walls of buildings and facing the parapets of the footbridge. Old favourites were 'Stephen's Ink', 'Swan Pens', 'Virol', 'O.X.O.' and 'Palethorpe's Sausages'.

Earlier types were far more attractive than their later counterparts, as they made use of cast iron base-plates and what was known as dry process enamelling. During the 1920s and 1930s steel was often substituted for iron, with 'spray-on' applications. The colours of the latter types, however, were not so bright or clear as those prepared by earlier techniques. Both could be chipped and crazed by small boys with stick and stones, although many cracked where there were pre-formed apertures for masonry nails, essential for fixing purposes.

Prize-winning van horses and drivers, in the cab-drive off Station Street. 1936. By kind permission of Mrs E Workman, whose husband was the police officer on the right of the picture.

Birmingham Post & Mail.

Although now staging a revival and often regarded as collector's items, they were greatly disliked by the prudish and austere planners of the post-Second World War era, disappearing long before the demolition of the old station. During the 1950s the sides of the overbridge and its inner parapets were divided into neat panels on which more conventional posters and signs were displayed, the general effect seeming prim and tasteful to the point of depression, a perfect example of 'ghastly good taste' in practice.

Modern planners were not alone in their dislike of early advertising schemes. It may be of interest to quote a letter to the *Birmingham Mail* of 1924, in which the writer complained that, "signs and advertisments spoil the station and block out light, especially on number four platform." New Street, Birmingham—like many other stations, was described as being, "at the mercy of the advertisers."

The Red Carpet Treatment

Claims are often made, in recording the history of a station, concerning the number of royal and distinguished visitors who deign to tread its platforms and receive the 'red carpet treatment'. New Street has certainly had its share of such visits, on both formal and informal occasions, too numerous to record within the limits of these pages. It has been a frequent practice, however, for a royal entourage visiting the area by rail to leave their train at Stechford, at the southern approaches to Birmingham, on the Euston-New Street main line, about four miles from the centre. Royal persons have also been known to reach New Street incognito, travelling in reserved carriages or compartments of ordinary expresses.

Holiday Traffic 1925

All records for holiday traffic were broken, especially from New Street, in July and August 1925. In addition to ordinary passengers and holiday-makers there were exceptionally large numbers of scouts, guides, cadets and territorials going to their annual or weekend camps, some in special trains. Many duplicate and triplicate services were introduced while some trains were quadrupled. On the 1st August, from 10 o'clock onwards, the Stephenson Place entrance was nearly impassable. Blackpool and the resorts in North Wales were the most popular destinations. There were, however, great difficulties and even dangers in coping with the crush, while some resorts reported 'full-up' long before the morning trains left their points of departure. At Blackpool, on the 3rd August, people were sharing police cells or sleeping in promenade shelters and on park benches. At Rhyl late-comers were directed straight from the station to the town hall and other public buildings, where temporary accommodation had been prepared on the dormitory-plan. Even the midnight trains were over-crowded and one starting from Coventry was not allowed to pick up any more passengers at New Street. Fortunately reserve trains could always be found.

Conditions were said to be even worse on the Midland side of the station. One man standing in the corridor of a holiday train complained that his jacket had been caught in the door. When the door was opened by a railway official, other people swarmed-in and there was difficulty in closing it before the train could start. Corridors were jammed to capacity while nearly all compartments had seventeen or eighteen people each. Some had scrambled through half-open windows, ignoring the protests of both platform staff and fellow travellers.

At a slightly later period when Blackpool introduced its season of illuminations, there were numerous evening excursions running from New Street. Most of these left about five o'clock in the afternoon returning at midnight. The fares were 5s return (old money). Many of the old North Western locomotives, in semi-retirement, were used on these trips, including some that looked as if they had been rescued from the scrapyard or cripple road. In the words of an ex-driver, "it's a wonder how some of them got through."

During the summer holiday period there were often special excursions for children, supervised by teachers and other volunteers. They would take whole train loads of young people to popular seaside resorts at greatly reduced prices, allowing them a few hours digging-up the beach or splashing in the sea, often when their parents were unable to provide longer holidays away from home. Most would arrive clutching buckets and spades, toy boats and packets of sandwiches, laughing and cheerful even when rain clouds darkened the horizon. Just getting away from the back streets and the novelty of a railway journey was enough for many of them.

A New Train Indicator

A new 'super' train indicator was erected just inside the station entrance in Stephenson Place in October 1926. It was claimed that, "one merely glanced at the bold destination headings to find a complete list of trains from midnight to midnight". There was also a special local side and a section for Sunday services. The apparatus had 4,136 slots for train times, with over thirty main line routes and about the same number of locals. The indicator was twenty five feet in length.

An Experimental Turbine Locomotive

According to a column in the *Birmingham Post* for the 4th April 1927, "A large, dull-grey engine in works livery had been spotted standing at number four platform on the previous day. This was "almost completely devoid of funnel, with squat lines, more continental than British" in outward appearance. There was also a distinct absence of smoke and puff. The locomotive was said to be undergoing tests in the Birmingham area, especially on the nearby Lickey Bank. It was a turbine-driven 2,000 h.p. locomotive with an overall weight of 140 tons and total length of 60ft, capable of 85 m.p.h. It had been constructed by Beyer-Peacock and Company, Limited, of Manchester (Gorton Works), to the patent-designs of L. Jungstrom. Although coal-fired it was economical to run and a great fuel-saver especially at high speeds. The tender or bunker was concealed within the bodywork at the rear-end of the locomotive, containing 16 tons of solid fuel. The wheels were small and uniform, like those of a later diesel locomotive, without valve gear or connecting rods. On this occasion it stood silently at the head of the 9.12 a.m. train for Derby, with fourteen coaches at the drawbar. It glided out of the station at the pressure of a lever, without noise, smoke or pollution of any kind.

61

The 'Royal Scot' Display

On the 14th December 1927 an engine of the new 'Royal Scot' Class was brought to Birmingham and displayed to the public at a bay platform in the ex-L.N.W.R. part of the station, known as the 'Coffeehouse Siding'. This was next to the Queen's drive where there had been a former refreshment room and canteen, later used as headquarters by the railway police. The presence of the locomotive had been announced by newspaper advertisements and banner-type posters spanning the Queen's Drive, also in other parts of the building. Admissions were 6d per head (old money) with children half-price, the aim being to raise money for local hospitals.

The version shown at New Street, for three days, was then un-named, but later christened *Lady of the Lake*. Its number was 6149, at that period painted on the tender sides in the style of the old Midland Railway. A visit to the viewing platform also included a conducted tour of the footplate, with full technical explanations by the driver, although the engine was not in steam, its fire being dropped for the duration of the exhibition. Some people were even allowed to enter the smoke box, in which the average adult could stand upright without difficulty.

Apart from such brief encounters the 'Scots' or '6-P' Class, mainly headed trains between London and Glasgow, using the Trent Valley line from Rugby, for which they were designed. They were seldom seen in any part of Birmingham, unless diverted due to track repairs, accidents or general maintenance on other lines.

LMS 4-6-0 'Royal Scot' class express locomotive. Introduced December 1927.

Bryan Holden Collection.

Trains Special and Otherwise

During the inter-war years all types of passenger trains ran through or to and from New Street, with extra workings for excursions and specials. There were, however, only two named expresses at this period. These were the 'Devonian' connecting with Torbay and the even better-known 'Pines Express'. 'The Pines' commenced running under this name in 1927, but was claimed to be a reintroduction of an L.N.W.R. express of the pre-war period, between Manchester and Bournemouth. Its name derived from the numerous pine trees found in parks and chines surrounding Bournemouth, which gave the district its pure air scented with pine needles. Locomotives on this train were usually changed at New Street, as were many others from all directions, with rare visitations from the previously mentioned 'Royal Scots' or the smaller 'Baby Scots' (also known as Patriots), at least from Manchester southwards. A named express known as the 'Midlander', ran between Euston and New Street during the period after the Second World War.

During the 1920s and 30s special trains ran over short distances to Bournville Station on the Gloucester line (former Birmingham and West Suburban Railway), as part of a conducted tour round the chocolate factory and garden village of that name, organised for publicity by Messrs Cadbury's Limited. Special coaching stock in a distinctive livery was reserved for these trips. In those days Cadburys made considerable use of both railway and canal transport, both the former Midland line and the Worcester and Birmingham Canal skirting their factory on the eastern side.

Looking towards Camp Hill, Brighton Road Station, as it was some 50 years ago. The engine is an LNWR 'Jumbo', presumably on a portion of the 'Pines Express'.

John Edgington Collection.

STANDARD 4-6-0 EXPRESS LOCOMOTIVE NO. 6126
"ROYAL SCOT" CLASS
LONDON, MIDLAND & SCOTTISH RAILWAY

When the heavy industries section of the British Industries Fair opened in specially designed buildings near Castle Bromwich Aerodrome, from the early 1930s, the L.M.S. ran frequent shuttle services over the Derby line via Saltley, to Castle Bromwich Station. These were push-and-pull trains usually handled by tank engines of the former North Staffordshire Railway. Special trains were also run to Bromford Bridge, between Castle Bromwich and Saltley, serving a halt connected with the now defunct Birmingham Race Course. The latter was only open on days when there was racing at Birmingham.

Filming at New Street

On the 25th June 1931 a special train arrived at New Street and was stabled first in the back sidings and later in the Coffehouse Bay. It consisted of several closed vans containing equipment for both filming and sound recording.

General train and station noises were recorded for the new talking picture, "Footsteps in the Night", which had a number of interesting railway sequences. In those days the 'talkies' were something of a novelty and much of the work was of a secret, experimental nature. Train running noises had also been recorded on the journey to Birmingham between Euston and New Street, and at Willesden Junction.

A considerable footage of background material was shot at New Street, at one point making use of a special passenger train hired for the purpose and crowded with extras. This was the first time such sequences had been shot live in a main line station, the L.M.S. keeping a special engine and rolling stock in reserve, to be used as needed. Most of the shots were taken on number one platform.

Midland compound heading a local train for Derby on the ex Midland side of New Street.

H C Stafford.

The Passenger's Friend

Over the Christmas period of 1932 an official was appointed at New Street known as 'The Passenger's Friend'. This was a Mr J. Hall, part of a new corps of platform staff officially known as 'L.M.S. Enquiry Inspectors', based on Birmingham, Liverpool, Manchester, Leeds and one or two other railway centres. The duty of these men was to answer questions, offering help and advice to passengers according to circumstances. Mr Hall was described in the local press as ideal for his job and "a model of tact and a mountain of patience." In order to make such people conspicuous and easy to find they were dressed in uniforms that would have made Beau Brummel, or even a modern pop star, look dowdy. The bright red coat and trousers were smothered in gold braid, while the peaked cap was also braided so that by many people Mr Hall was often mistaken for a field marshal or the visiting head of some friendly Latin American Republic. A few of the less sophisticated passengers may have been too awe-stricken to approach him and passed with bowed heads or token salutations.

The First Main Line Diesel.

The first single unit diesel-electric passenger-carrying railcar came in 1933. This operated an experimental service between London (Euston), New Street and the British Industries Fair at Castle Bromwich. It arrived in Birmingham after a trial run via Rugby, on the 14th February, its passengers being distinguished guests of the inaugurating company.

The unit — known as a train — travelled at exceptional speed and saving in fuel costs, arriving exactly on time. For a journey of 113 miles, 25 gallons of fuel oil were needed at a cost of 8d per mile (old money). It was officially known as the 'Armstrong-Shell Express' and had been constructed and designed by Sir W. G. Armstrong-Whitworth in co-operation with Shell-Mex, B.P. Limited and the L.M.S. It was propelled by its own electrical power, generated by a 250 b.h.p Armstrong Whitworth Diesel engine, having a cruising speed of 58 m.p.h. While working to and from the B.I.F. it made use of a special station or platform at Castle Bromwich, designed for its sole use.

The 'Royal Scot' Train

In January 1934 the 'Royal Scot' engine and train arrived in New Street, where it was on display for a short period, after its successful 11,000 miles tour of North America. Birmingham was to be the first provincial city it would honour in this way before making a nation-wide journey, finally returning to normal service between Euston and Glasgow. It had previously been shipped to the United States for the 'Century of Progress' Exhibition, held in Chicago. It subsequently travelled in both the U.S. and Canada visiting eighty cities and towns and being inspected by 3,021,607 people. This was eight years after the visit to New Street of the 'Royal Scot' engine *Lady of the Lake,* previously described.

This time there was not only a locomotive and tender but eight corridor coaches, making up a train identical with the one running in America. It included an all-electric kitchen car, a sleeping car, first class lounge-car and several items of ordinary passenger stock.

During its stay in Birmingham the 'Royal Scot' train occupied a bay of number one platform, protected by barriers decorated with flags and bunting of red, white and blue. The crew included Driver William Gilbertson, who had been in charge of the footplate throughout the tour and was eventually awarded the British Empire Medal in the New Year's Honours List. He was supported at New Street by Fireman John Jackson and Fitter Clifford Woods, both of whom had taken part in the American tour. Driver Gilbertson had 47 years of railway service to his credit, mainly on the footplates of passenger locomotives. The show lasted for two days and could be viewed between the hours of 10 a.m. and 10 p.m. On its arrival the train and its crew were given a civic welcome by the Lord Mayor of Birmingham, Alderman H. E. Goodby. Many other local dignitaries were present including the Mayors of West Bromwich and Walsall. The exhibition was seen by 43,749 people.

The Harborne Closure

As a result of the grouping there were several closures of the less important suburban stations and routes, although a fair number remained until after the Second World War. Sadly missed was the Wolverhampton-Walsall service (via Short Heath) of the former Midland Railway, ending in 1931.

Perhaps an even greater loss, tinged with sentiment and regret, was the closure, to passenger traffic, of a short branch between the pleasant suburb of Harborne, where there was a small terminus, and the L.N.W.R. side of New Street in 1934. The 'Harborne Express', as it was nicknamed by generations of commuters, schoolboys and train-spotters, usually ran from a bay on number one platoform, formerly reserved for Stour Valley traffic. A line was opened to Harborne in 1874 and also served a coal wharf near Hagley Road and three other passengers stations at Icknield Port Road, Hagley Road and Rotton Park Road. Icknield Port Road was little used and closed on the 18th May 1931. There were also exchange sidings for what was long claimed to be the world's largest brewery, at Cape Hill, having a junction for an extensive private railway near Rotton Park Road. Journey time was about twenty two minutes, normally with two or three coach trains handled by ex-L.N.W.R. tank engines. Goods and mineral traffic remained on the line until the Beeching axe fell, in November 1963. In recent years the lines were lifted and their pathway untilised as an urban nature trail.

This had always been a popular line with regular passengers, used by businessmen, school-children and shoppers for a period of over sixty years. Everyone seemed to know everyone else and many of the locals were holders of season tickets. Drivers, firemen and guards were always greeted with a cheery word. The return fare was only 3d (old money). There were many protests at the closure but local services had been undermined by the increased number of motorbuses on all routes and the ownership of private cars. Main line traffic was always given precedence at Harborne Junction, with the Stour Valley line, which could lead to late running and numerous complaints on this score, becoming a music hall joke and the subject matter for comic postcards.

The last outward run before passenger closure, was reported in the *Birmingham Mail* for the 26th November 1934. There appear to have been large crowds on the platform and many well-wishers. "The last Harborne Express left New Street at 11 p.m. on Saturday night. It was packed with regular passengers and season ticket holders . . . seen off by Mr J. R. Brook, the District Passenger Manager, on behalf of the Company. There were loud cheers from crowds collected on the platforms at Monument Lane, Rotton Park and Hagley Road Stations. Paper streamers were loosed from compartment windows at several points along the track. On arriving at the terminus everyone seemed determined to shake the driver and fireman by the hand, while others stole lumps of coal as souvenirs." Flash-light photographs were taken and people of all ages swarmed over the tracks. There were cries of 'Speech', 'Speech' but no-one responded and the station master seems to have experienced great difficulty in closing the building and clearing the area.

Last passenger train on the Harborne Branch (4 November 1963) surrounded by photographers and enthusiasts near Harborne Station.

Harborne Public Library.

The Press-Button Time Table.

This was a device first brought into use in 1936. There were eventually two such machines, one at the entrance from Stephenson Place and the other on the bridge near platform four. In appearance they resembled the push-button machines found on the London Underground for ticket vending. They each had a window like a television screen, through which could be seen the names of a large number of stations. Each station was numbered and below the window was a keyboard bearing corresponding numbers to the stations on the list. An enquirer pressed the button relating to the station about which information was sought, and a card slid down bearing full details including times, changes and alternative routes.

The Birmingham Centenaries

The year 1937 marked the centenary of the London to Birmingham train service. The through route via Kilsby Tunnel, however, was not opened until a year later. To mark the celebrations there was an exhibition of early documents, books and pictures at the Science Museum, South Kensington.

There was a further exhibition in 1938 and the announcement that a London to Birmingham express would be run known as the 'Centenary Special'. On the day of the 17th September, to mark the opening of the line throughout, there was a special menu in the dining cars of all expresses between Euston and New Street, with souvenir menu-cards. A Centenary Exhibition in Birmingham was visited by 25,000 people. A small selection of early coaches and locomotives were on display at Euston. On the 15th November there was a banquet at Grosvenor House, London, at which the guest of honour was the then Duke of Gloucester.

LNWR express locomotive, No 790 Hardwicke, *which distinguished itself in the famous 1895 race to Scotland between west and east coast routes. New Street Centenary Exhibition, 1st June 1954.*

Naming the 'Royal Warwickshire Regiment'.

On the 27th June 1938, the L.M.S. named their engine No. 6131 after the Royal Warwickshire Regiment. The act of naming was performed by Brigadier C. T. Tomes D.S.O., Colonel of the regiment, in a ceremony on platform one at New Street. The engine was one of the 'Royal Scot' Class of which there were seventy one in service, many bearing the names of regiments or corps of the British Army. There was a military guard of honour at the approaches to the platform, which had also been decorated with flags and national emblems. The Lord Mayor of Birmingham was an honoured guest while Mr William (later Sir William) Stanier—Chief Mechanical Engineer of the L.M.S.—acted as host. The engine was in the care of Driver A. Paddock and Fireman P. Munn, both of whom were Birmingham men and former members of the Royal Warwickshire Regiment,

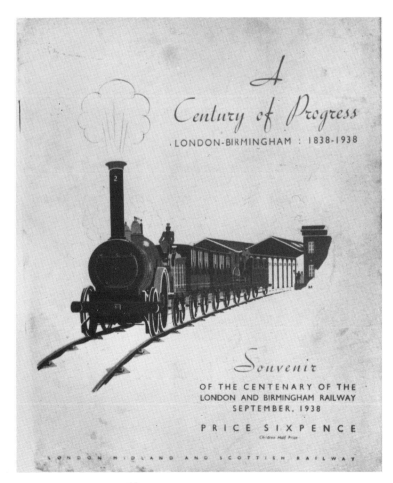

Souvenire booklet of the London and Birmingham Railway Centenary, 1838-1938.

Bryan Holden Collection.

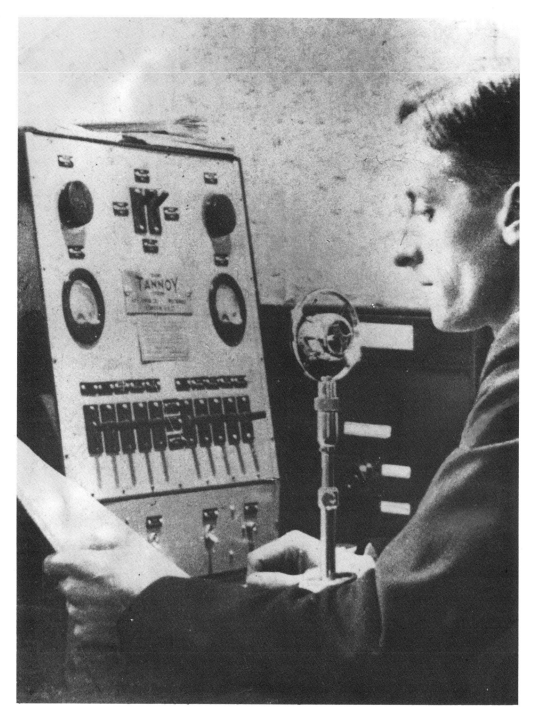

Train Announcers.

In 1935 a system of internal broadcasting was installed at New Street, which became one of the first British main line stations to use controlled loud-speakers for train and other announcements. This proved useful not only as a guide to bewildered travellers but to reunite divided families or missing friends and find mislaid parcels or luggage. People were even warned that known cardsharpers were seen boarding certain trains, with full explanations as to why certain services were delayed. In cases of sudden illness doctors or trained nurses could be summoned quickly.

It was an announcement on the loud-speakers that made it possible for a complete Coventry City football team to play an away game against Sheffield United. Fog on the line had disrupted services to such an extent that most of the players found it impossible to reach New Street, where they were meeting their team captain, then living in Birmingham, in time for their planned connection. An S.O.S. at New Street brought the captain, George Mason, to the telephone and later relaid information concerning alternative routes over the former Great Central line via Rugby. Instructions were phoned back to Coventry and all the players were eventually reunited, not only in time for the match but for a comfortable lunch in Sheffield.

At first the broadcasts ended during the late evening, but eventually they were continuous throughout a twenty four four period. The idea had been mooted by the station master Mr J. Harrison, who made the first announcements to open the service. The microphone was later shared by Mr F.M. Easton and Mr D. Hedges with a Mr T. Varty assisting during holiday periods. The first woman announcer came during the wartime period in 1941. By 1940 there was a team of six regular announcers. All had been chosen for their sound diction, clear accents and friendly manner. According to an article in the *Daily Sketch* "B.B.C. announcers must look to their laurels. In Birmingham there are golden microphone voices so cultured and distinct that they would easily take first prizes against Broadcasting House in open competition. "The train now standing at platform six leaves for . . ." rings out the stentorian voice and comfortable assurance comes to passengers, regulars and strangers alike, at New Street Station."

The announcers were not specially trained, but were gifted spokesmen drawn from the uniformed staff of the railway. Their cultured voices, minus any suggestion of the 'Bermingum' dialect, made them many friends. They had a huge fan mail and only one complaint seems to have been made. The single dissident was Miss Lyn Fairclough, a telephone operator, whose bedroom overlooked the station. While she could get used to the trains and other station noises the loud-speakers, rumbling and booming at frequent intervals, often prevented her from enjoying a sound night's sleep.

Frank Easton, the first train announcer at New Street Station. 1935.

Permission F Easton.

71

*At the height of the Birmingham
blitz, New Street Station was
badly hit on a number of
occasions. The domed roof on the
LNWR side was a victim of
incendiary attack in July 1942.*

4.
Second World War
—and after

During the Second World War people, especially civilians, were discouraged from travelling 'unless absolutely necessary'.

There were staff shortages and food shortages so that elderly people could no longer depend on assistance with their luggage or hungry travellers expect nourishing meals or even a snack in the refreshment rooms, although most service trains had been deprived of their dining and buffet cars. At night the station was blacked-out, with shaded lamps, and even the waiting rooms were shrouded in gloom. After blackout-time all trains had to keep their blinds down and doors leading into corridors could not be left open, even in the warmest weather; matters which were constantly checked by porters, guards and ticket collectors. The cabs of steam engines had to be sheeted-up at top and sides, the sheets kept in rolls strapped to the roof during daylight hours.

Platform edges, the heads of steps, projections and low archways were painted white, but even these precautions could not prevent a few nasty accidents. The width of white strips along platform edges was usually between a foot and six inches. Glass windows in the station area were covered with criss-cross patterns of tape and sticky paper to prevent them shattering in heat or explosions. Some of the more important doors and windows were protected by brick anti-blast walls or barricades of sandbags. While a large quantity of the glass was taken from the domed roofs, whole sections in both parts of the station were covered with layers of hessian sacking, which at the end of the war took nearly eight months to remove.

Large numbers of servicemen and women were once more in evidence, with even greater numbers of foreign and Colonial or Commonwealth troops, many wearing unfamiliar uniforms and speaking strange languages.

Many seemed bewildered and unsure of themselves, glad to be directed to the N.A.A.F.I. canteen or even to the makeshift headquarters of the Railway Transport Officer. The N.A.A.F.I. canteen was on number one platform, converted from a former cloak room and left luggage office. There was also a Y.M.C.A. canteen near the entrance to the Queen's Drive in Worcester Street. A 24-hour rest centre for women travellers, especially service women and those engaged in war work, was opened in 1943, at 61 Station Street, on the Midland side.

One of the saddest sights at New Street, during the early days of the war, was the evacuation of young children from Birmingham to areas well away from the likelihood of enemy bombing. They were taken by special trains from platforms at both New Street and Snow Hill, each with a small suitcase, a packed meal and tiny gasmask in a square cardboard box. Some were almost too young to be parted from their parents and dreaded that they were seeing the last of all they had formerly known and loved.

The main line railway companies in Britain were well prepared for the outbreak of war. There had been a year of crisis and international tension in 1938, which at least gave the country a chance to prepare for action. Railway staff in all grades had been encouraged to take part in training for air raid precautions, fire fighting, rescue work and first aid. Many railway workers were issued with steel helmets while footplatemen also had service-type respirators, anti-gas gauntlets and special boots. Porters and platform staff had to give up using hand lamps and were issued with small electric torches.

Station staff in reserved occupations or too old for active service, frequently volunteered for part-time Home Guard, Auxiliary Fire Service and A.R.P. duties. Nearly everyone was expected to sacrifice a night of each week fire-watching either at their home or place of work. This frequently meant turns in dangerous or exposed places, watching for the small incendiary bombs, which given the right training, were easy enough, to control, but more deadly than high explosives if the fires they started were allowed to spread. The Railway Home Guard was at first without weapons or uniforms. It patrolled and guarded bridges, junctions and other key points, the members wearing armbands with ordinary clothes and drilling with broomsticks until enough rifles could be supplied.

People caught in New Street during an air raid were given warnings over the loud-speakers and told to shelter in the numerous subways. Others were shepherded by the platform staff into waiting rooms and other suitable places. Those remaining in carriages were advised to lie on the floor or squeeze under seats, covering themselves with any available coats and rugs. Any cover was desirable, if only as protection against flying glass, while unnecessary movements that might hinder communications and delay rescue-work were greatly deplored. No one was allowed to shelter in the tunnels.

Birmingham was badly hit over a prolonged period by German night bombing, and there was considerable damage in and around the station areas at both New Street and Snow Hill. The first important casualty was number five signal box, which was half demolished and put out of action on the 16th October 1940. This was followed, a few days later, by the almost complete destruction of the District Control Centre, which had to transfer to the protection of a bomb-proof shelter, although operating for at least twelve months in cramped conditions of extreme stress and chaos.

Several high-explosive bombs were dropped on the west side of the station during the night of the 26th October 1940, causing damage beyond the scope of ordinary railwaymen to clear away in a short time. Station staff struggled manfully, but had to be reinforced by large numbers of soldiers and other servicemen. This caused the station to be closed for a period of twenty four hours.

An unexploded bomb of the delayed action type was known to have been dropped in the Queen's Drive, on the 20th November 1940. The station was first evacuated and closed, but reopened several hours later as it was thought the bomb had blown-up of its own accord. It was re-discovered on the 13th March 1942, during other excavations, and promptly defused by the Royal Engineers.

On the 19th November number four signal box was badly damaged and eventually destroyed, while many glass windows of the Queen's Hotel were shattered by blast, despite earlier precautions. Damage in the area was so serious that operations in and out of New Street were suspended from the 19th to the 21st November.

Tunnels were blocked by high explosive bombs on the 10th April 1941, the south tunnel being closed for four days and the west tunnel for eight days. Numerous incendiary bombs were dropped on New Street and Curzon Street, especially on the night of the 28th July 1942, badly affecting the domed roof on the L.N.W.R. side of New Street.

One of the casualties during the 1940 air raids was the so-called New Street Institute in the station buildings, which had celebrated its golden jubilee in 1935. This was a social club for railway workers with a membership of over two hundred. Its aim was to provide relaxation in off-duty hours, with billiards, table tennis, darts and light refreshments. It was reopened in new quarters just over two years later.

When the Americans came into the war this had a considerable effect on New Street traffic and operations. Thousands of American G.I.'s, were stationed at barracks and encampments near Lichfield and to the north of Birmingham, some at Whittington Barracks (formerly the depot of the North

Steps leading to the public footbridge from the Station Street booking office. There were identical staircases on either side of the booking office. Date uncertain, but may have been taken in wartime, with sign indicating R.T.O. office on platform 1.

Birmingham Post & Mail.

Staffordshire Regiment) while others took possession of a large housing estate at Great Barr, from which the tenants had been evacuated as a wartime measure. Stores and supplies were shipped via New Street to Sutton Coldfield, where they were collected in army trucks, New Street serving as a staging post and Sutton Coldfield as the railhead. The station in Sutton Park was an important centre for collecting and forwarding U.S. mail.

This mail was kept apart from G.P.O. deliveries, brought mainly from ports on the south coast such as Southampton and Plymouth and delivered in special mail vans reserved for the purpose. Special engines at Birmingham were also kept in reserve to deal with this traffic. Troops were frequently detrained on platform three at New Street under the supervision of their own M.P.s, trucks and jeeps gaining access to the platform area from the Queen's Drive. American troops were noted for their generosity, especially to children and those appearing less fortunate than themselves. They would frequently fling packets of sweets, chewing gum and cigarettes through carriage windows whilst on their way to ports of embarkation.

Throughout the war numerous troop and hospital trains came to New Street. There were also important movements of naval personnel to and from Scottish ports. A large variety of engines from other companies and regions were to be seen, especially from the G.W.R. and the L.N.E.R. Most hospital trains came from the south, some of the patients being taken off at New Street for special treatment in Birmingham hospitals. During the unloading of stretcher cases more light than usual was allowed and the blackout regulations eased for the sake of the wounded.

Midland 'Compound' leaving platform 1, during the 1930s.

G. R. Moyle.

Bridge Rebuilding

Important bridge repair and rebuilding operations commenced at New Street during the early 1940s. This mainly concerned roads over the north western end of the station at Hill Street and Navigation Street. The original Hill Street bridge had been constructed nearly a hundred years earlier and, although strengthened from time-to-time, was not intended for the rapidly increasing weight of modern traffic. There was also a limit to the amount of patching-up operations, especially in wartime. By 1943 a new and extensive survey had been made and it was decided to rebuild the entire structure, also to rebuild or renovate the Navigation Street bridge. The first stage, at Hill Street, was to make a temporary bridge in parallel with the old structure, having a 12ft carriageway and a pavement or pedestrian way on one side only. This was supported on the underside by sturdy wooden trestles and a number of secondhand girders, able to take considerable strain and weight, if only for a temporary period. Yet because of the sharp right-hand turn at the lower end, its continued use was considered too dangerous in blackout conditions or during air raids. It was finally blocked to all traffic and construction work ceased until after the war, recommencing early in 1948 and completed in 1951.

The Midland side at New Street, looking towards Hill Street.

Photo: Reg Hollins
Permission Westwood Press

The Navigation Street bridge was not completed until 1953, being a larger structure than the one in Hill Street, with a clear width between parapets of 60ft, while the permanent roadway at Hill Street was only 42ft.

'City of Birmingham'

On the 20th March 1945 there was an interesting ceremony that helped to bring a touch of glamour to the old station. It began at 11.15 a.m. on a crisp day in early spring when the sleek bulk of a 'Coronation' Class locomotive slid into New Street. It was a Pacific 4-6-2 type (streamlined) weighing 164 tons and measuring 74ft., including tender. On arriving at New Street it had run 407,110 miles in revenue service. It had been constructed, with others of its class, in 1939 and mainly worked in express passenger service between Euston and Glasgow, being the first engine of its type to enter New Street.

On the 19th February it had been taken to Aston shed and given various tests to make sure that it could run into the Birmingham station without damaging itself or the platform facings. It was then removed to the paint shops at Crewe and refurbished for a naming ceremony to be held at New Street, the following month. The crew on this occasion were both local men, being Driver H. G. Barr from Stockland Green and Fireman J. E. Schuck of Witton. Mr Barr had been on the railways twenty five years. Both were ex-servicemen, Mr Barr having won the Military Medal on the Somme during the First World War, while Mr Schuck had served with the Royal Engineers during the earlier part of the Second World War.

79

When the streamlined 'Pacific' rolled into New Street it was arrayed in the unlined black livery adopted by all locomotives during this period. This was very different from the silver and blue or scarlet and gold worn by sister engines at the time of building. Apart from its normal express duties, the engine had worked to a limited extent in mixed traffic and hauling troop trains over the West Coast route to Scotland, its normal loading being 540 tons tare. Working on the pre-war 'Coronation Scot Express' it covered 401 miles between London and Glasgow in $6^1/_2$ hours, and was capable of maximum speeds of 90 m.p.h. During a test run, a record speed of 114 m.p.h. had been attained, by an almost identical locomotive of the same class.

Later in the day, at a ceremony presided over by the Lord Mayor of Birmingham (Alderman W.H. Wiggins-Davies) — the engine was christened *City of Birmingham'*. It was the first 'Coronation Scot' Class locomotive to be named after a city or town. Among others present were the Acting Lady Mayoress and Lord Roydon, the latter being Chairman of the L.M.S., appearing on behalf of the company.

The locomotive was withdrawn from service in 1964. It had clocked-up 1,650,000 miles but was still in excellent and roadworthy condition. It was later presented to the Birmingham Museum of Science and Industry, but not for immediate display, as the museum was undergoing a rebuilding programme that lasted six years. From 1966 until 1972 *City of Birmingham* was kept on an open plot of land next to the museum, protected by waterproof covers. A new locomotive hall, now shared with other vintage transport, was literally built over and round the main exhibit. After the war the locomotive's streamlined casing had been removed and it received a new livery of British Railway's green, lined-out in black and orange. It now appears in its final colour scheme, moving backwards and forwards over a short length of ballasted permanent way (propelled by a concealed electric motor) to demonstrate the working of rods and motion.

Platform Changes

There was an announcement to the general public on the 7th October, 1946 that platform numbers would be rearranged at New Street throughout. The original number one platform was to have five numbers. The two bay platforms at the London end were to become numbers one and two, while those at the Wolverhampton end were to be 1a and 2a. The main line platform, facing platform two, would be renumbered as three.

The ends of the island platform (originally number two) would become four and five respectively. The earlier platform three would be changed to number six and platform four renumbered as platform seven. The two sides of number five were to be renumbered eight and nine and the main line platform six renumbered ten, with its bay platform as number eleven.

Nationalisation

Shortly after the end of the Second World War, in 1948, the main line railways of Britain, then known as the 'Big Four', were nationalised and brought under the control of the Railway Executive. The privately owned companies were absorbed into various regions, New Street becoming an important centre of the London Midland Region. By this time very little had been done to repair the ravages of enemy action and wartime neglect; what had been achieved was mainly classed as patching-up routines.

Prior to the outbreak of war the main line companies had been greatly hampered in their development by outmoded legislation and other difficulties, not of their making, that hindered them when fighting back against encroachments of modern road traffic. Large posters urging the government to 'Give the Railways a Square Deal', were seen outside every station in the country during the late 1930s. Perhaps some of the largest and most impressive appeared on hoardings near the entrance to the Queen's Drive in Navigation Street. Yet government aid and concern came with strings attached and even before the end of the war there was a rumour that wartime control might be extended in the guise of radical legislation. Perhaps the London Midland sector buckled-down and accepted their new circumstances with a better grace than their rival groups in private enterprise, if only to make the most of what many regarded as inevitable.

Shunting vans into former carriage loading bay — an extension to platform 6. 12 June 1958.

M Mensing.

8.5 am to Newcastle-on-Tyne leaving platform 7, headed by Stanier Class '5' 4-6-0 No 44964. 29 June 1957.

M Mensing.

When nationalised the station at New Street was regarded as one of the largest in Britain. In the immediate post-war period 190 trains came into the station per day. The operating staff could cope with eight trains in the station at any given time, while men and women in full-time employment numbered 800. There were over $10^1/_4$ million passengers per annum. Refreshment rooms or buffets were still to be found on all platforms except number two, later renumbered four and five. There were eventually book stalls or news stands on all platforms, except on number two, originally controlled by W.H. Smith and Sons but later by Wyman's Limited.

Reconstruction and Demolition

In 1948 vital work commenced on the reconstruction of the Hill Street road bridge and later of the Navigation Street bridge — as previously mentioned — which took priority over other schemes.

Another work of great importance, commenced the same year was the dismantling of the single-span roof on the former L.N.W.R. side. This had been strengthened and renovated earlier in the century but was severely damaged in wartime air raids to become a battered wreck. Bombs and blast had taken their toll with very little of the original structure intact and the remaining parts unsafe. No attempt had been made to paint or even repatch any part of the structure since a year or two before the outbreak of the Second World War, apart from stripping-off certain hessian cloth covers. To restore fully the roof and keep it in good order for a minimum period of twenty years would have cost more than was thought expedient. As an alternative, a new umbrella-type roofing, or series of roofs, were introduced. Even before the war many passengers complained that the glass roof was almost obscured by grime and that it leaked badly in several places.

Dismantling the old roof, then ninety four years old and weighing 900 tons, was almost as much of a task as its original construction, even taking into account the extent of wartime damage. The work was carried out under the supervision of Mr W.K. Wallace, Chief Engineer of the L.M.S. and later of the London Midland Region of B.R., assisted by a local staff team. The first trusses were removed from the London end, each truss supported on a temporary scaffolding of tubular steel. Each truss was cut by oxy-acetylene torches and reduced to pieces small enough for scrap-disposal. As in the construction work, a type of movable bridge was eventually used, later joined by a second bridge or gantry, both designed in solid steel and supplied by the Darlaston (Staffordshire) firm of Rubery Owen and Company Limited. Most of the work was carried-out by the Altitude Contracting Company of Birmingham. The span of the bow-string girders had been 212ft at the Wolverhampton end and 191ft at the London end.

The new umbrella roofing was a simple construction of steel cross-girders, that formed separate awnings on each platform and above the footbridge. Above the basic framework were corrugated asbestos sheets with clear perspex sheets on a ratio of one to four. At platform level the sheeting overhung the tracks by at least 2ft on each side. The clock and signal box on the footbridge were also removed at this period. Electric lighting was now used as the main source of illumination, with sychronised electric clocks on all platforms.

The so-called 'Paxton Roofs' on the Midland side of the station, constructed as a double-span unit, were not affected by these changes and remained until total rebuilding during the 1960s. Most would admit that more air and light were brought into the station on the L.N.W.R. side as a whole, but few could deny that low awnings above the footbridge had a cramping and claustrophobic effect, while much of the cathedral-like atmosphere had also vanished.

LMS 'Jubilee' 4-6-0, No 45651 Shovell, *arriving at platform 9 with the 12.52 pm York — Bristol.* 0-6-0 No 44553 *(light engine) on the right.*

M Mensing.

Later Changes

During the late 1940s and early 1950s there were several minor developments in the station area, some admirable and other less so, roughly divided between a matter of taste and needless expediture. On the credit side there were new stands for sheet time tables on certain platforms. There were vast repainting and redecorating schemes that took at least two years, while new clocks were provided on the Stephenson Street side of the station and on all platforms. Lighting was improved on the footbridge and there were modern train departure indicators.

Less pleasing but perhaps necessary economies, were the rebuilding of two refreshment rooms as self-service cafeterias and the redesigning or streamlining of all booking offices, which seemed to destroy their more interesting architectural features. A large sign, displaying the name of the station in the acid colours of neon-lighting, by no means harmonising with its early Victorian architecture, straddled the facade in Stephenson Place, giving it more the appearance of a cinema than a main line station.

The 'Midlander'

On the 25th October 1950 it was announced that a new restaurant car express would run between Euston, Coventry, New Street and Wolverhampton. This was to be known as the 'Midlander'. Its scheduled running times would be Monday to Friday inclusive, taking two hours forty minutes in each direction. There were slower train timings than in pre-war days, due to the neglect and comparatively poor condition of the trackwork. The first train arrived in New Street at 11.00 a.m. to be accorded a civic reception by the Lord Mayor of Birmingham. It was headed by a rebuilt 'Royal Scot' Class engine, *King's Royal Rifle Corps*, in the care of Driver Thorpe. The train of eleven coaches, appeared in the new livery of 'blood and custard', adopted since nationalisation. This was to become the fastest steam-hauled express running between Euston and New Street in post-war years.

The New Street Centenary

Celebrations for this event began during May 1954 and continued well into the following month. Among other events a local rail tour was organised by the Stephenson Locomotive Society, several pamphlets were published and there was a three-day exhibition of locomotives and rolling stock in the station itself.

Seats on the 'S.L.S. Special' were sold out within two days of their advertisement, so that a duplicate trip was arranged for the following week. This was to be a three coach train hauled by one of the oldest locomotives available, which was an 0-6-2 tank engine built at Crewe in 1885. It covered the L.N.W.R. circle line from New Street via Perry Barr and Soho Road, then worked over the ex-G.W.R. junction at Smethwick to reach the Old Hill-Longbridge line, returning via Camp Hill and Saltley, running back to New Street over the old Midland circle through King's Heath and Selly Oak.

The exhibition at New Street was opened by the Lord Mayor on the 1st June 1954. It included the following items:-

Midland Railway coach. Non-corridor 3rd class. Built 1910.

2. L.N.W.R. coach. Corridor 3rd class. Built 1908.
3. Queen Victoria's saloon coach. This was originally designed and constructed as two vehicles, each of 30ft length, later gangwayed together. In 1895 the twin coaches were converted to a single coach of 60ft length, running on six-wheel bogies.
4. Queen Adelaide's saloon coach. This was built for the Dowager Queen Adelaide, consort of William IVth, in 1842.
5. Kirtley Locomotive No. 20002. Designed by Matthew Kirtley, later of the Midland Railway, who drove the first train into London, after the opening of the L. & B.R. It had a 2-4-0 wheel arrangement and weighed 62 tons 5 cwts, in working order.
6. *Hardwicke*. A locomotive of the L.N.W.R. 'Precedent' Class, being a 2-4-0 tender engine, then kept at Crewe in full working order. Built by F.W. Webb in 1892 and taking part in the celebrated railway race to Scotland in 1895.

7. No 46235, *City of Birmingham*. A 4-6-2 express locomotive designed by Stanier, previously named at New Street on the 20th March 1945. It was later stripped of its streamlined casing and presented with new name plates, also a version of the civic arms of Birmingham, unveiled by Alderman W.H. Wiggins-Davies.

The above abridged notes are taken from a small guide to the exhibition published by the London, Midland Region of British Railways. British Railways also published a paperback booklet on *The Story of New Street* by F.W. Grocott, issued to "commemorate the centenary of the opening of Birmingham, New Street Station, 1st June 1854". This ran to 16 pages with numerous illustrations. The Stephenson Locomotive Society (Midlands area group) also published a useful Railway History and Chronology of the West Midlands, to coincide with the Birmingham centenary.

No 46235 City of Birmingham, *at New Street Centenary, June 1954.*

R S Potts.

5

Recollections

The following pages consist mainly of quotes from people who knew the old station and have been kind enough to share their memories.

According to Mr F.A. Jones of Weoley Castle "Like many people of my age (I am now getting on for seventy), New Street Station is remembered with affection. Snow Hill seemed to be slightly upper crust and perhaps snooty, by comparison. It was always cleaner as no dust or dirt could survive the howling gales that drove along the platforms, especially when the north winds swept unobstructed into the wide-open end of the station... Agreed, New Street was smoky and noisy, but to my mind it had the warmth and comfort of a well-worn pair of slippers.

"One of my great memories was coming home on leave during the last war. I had been overseas for the better part of three years. The train was jolting along with the blinds down, but I figured we were not far out of Birmingham. I heard the engine give a whistle, and through the windows came the one and only smell of a New Street tunnel, there was no mistaking it, I was home! I would not have traded the smell of soot, steam and smoke for all the perfumes of Araby. The train stopped at platform six and I walked into the Queen's Drive."

Mr Jones spent much of his spare time as a schoolboy engine spotting with his pals, frequently making use of steps that led into the north western throat of the station from Pinfold Street. Here there was an uninterrupted view of the turntable across the running tracks. "We would watch with bated breath as the locomotives eased their way to dead centre, and the crew would strain with long handles at each end of the turntable so that the great machines revolved to the desired positions. It was a never failing marvel to us."

Perhaps Mr Jones did not realise that locomotives backing against the grade, over a slimy surface sometimes ended not on the table but in the empty pit.' He continues, "We would watch the trains, locals and expresses, work in and out, taking names and numbers. Boy-like, we would envy those gods in grimy overalls who, at the touch of a lever controlled and drove those magnificent maroon monsters. As they pulled away from the platform, they would pass under the bridge of Navigation Street, the funnel's blast hitting the roof-arch and clouding the loco' with a shroud of swirling steam; when the cylinders were being blown out, all you could see was the top half of the smokebox purposely driving forward. As the bridge was cleared, the steam blast shot triumphantly high in the air, billowing over Navigation Street. At times, with heavy rain, the driving wheels slipped; the loco' seemed to bellow frantically, until the sand gave the wheels extra grip, and it resumed its steady, powerful beat."

Mr Jones further records how he, "later worked for an electrical firm responsible for two signs in the station... along the footbridge, towards

Class '5' 4-6-0 No 44944 on the Midland side. April 24 1962.

C Chadwick.

93

Stephenson Place... Straddling the tracks and platforms on the former L.N.W.R. side, was a small signal box. Access was from the bridge via an iron ladder through a trapdoor. The cabin was open-topped, but surmounted by a large public clock, which in later years was further crowned by a blue neon sign proclaiming *'Hercules... the World's Best Cycle'*... At the end of the bridge a flight of shallow steps with a handrail in the middle, went up under an arch, which bore a further sign with the legend *'Drages... Bull Street'* (this appears to have been a local furniture store) in gold helium tubing, spread across its sweep.

"New Street had a rich odour... a compound of dust, smoke and steam-oil, all blended into an unforgettable aroma. The smell distilled-out into a kind of dirt or grime that settled everywhere it could get a hold, and when it was disturbed!... Our firm looked after the signs, as previously mentioned, and I used to give a loud groan when Len, with whom I worked said, "Frank, the Hercules or Drages' sign is up the spout"... We would get a ladder, if it was Drages, and man-handle it above the stonework of the arch and behind the rear panel, to get at the trouble. As soon as wires or tubes were touched there was quite a cloud of black, sooty dust. With your arms in a vertical position for work, it went up the sleeves, causing great discomfort. To reach the clock and switches was an acrobatic feat of no mean skill. It was one foot on the handrail, a quick grab upwards, the other foot where you might get a toehold and a quick scramble to the top of the arch. Like most electrical machinery, the converter had to be maintained and checked, needing constant attention. First the cover would be lifted off, gently — so that the layer of dust on the top had as little disturbance as possible, then the brushes examined and the copper carbon dust cleared away. This used to fly straight up my nose, and as I wiped my streaming nose and eyes, the grime on my hands transferred to my handkerchief, and from there back to my nose and across my face.

"The Hercules sign was not quite so bad. It was above the signal cabin but the top was open to the four winds and plenty of dirt. The cabin was in the centre of the bridge with levers at each end overlooking the platforms and rails. On the inside, round the base of the clock, was a long seat with a stove and signalling instruments. There was only one signalman at a time in the box, the work being in shifts. We got to know most of the signalmen and had some pleasant times there when things were a bit slack, but if things were hectic there was a fair chance we would be given our marching orders and asked to leave... the kettle was always on the stove, while the tea was sometimes so strong it had to be chewed.

"One day I was clearing up inside the sign with a hand-brush as part of a routine check. I had to get rid of the dust somehow and looked for the easiest way to get shut of it. I saw a small hole in the base of the sign and figured the clock would not mind (being directly underneath), and swept the dirt through. All at once there was a blasphemous cry, the dirt had gone through the clock, which was partly hollow, and was delicately topping a can of tea on the stove. The signalman expressed himself at great length but all went quiet at last and we carried on with our work. Shortly afterwards there was a smell of burning rubber, which nearly always meant panic stations. With neon

Ex-LMS 1600 hp diesel-electric Co-Co No 10000, leaving platform 1 with the 2.30 pm to Euston. 1 December 1956.

M Mensing.

Ex LMS 'Patriot' 4-6-0, No 45548 Lytham St Annes, 12.15 pm ex-Blackpool, (N) arriving at platform 3. 9 September 1959. In the top of the picture can be seen the remains of a fence and party wall between the station and former grammar school.

M Mensing.

signs and their high voltage this was a sure sign of trouble or danger. We rooted everywhere and the odour came and went, sometimes strong and sometimes faint, until we found the signalman with a satisfied grin on his face burning fragments of waste rubber in his stove and causing the panic . . . Was it in revenge for the spoilt brew?

A Mrs Kellett (nee Leadbetter) of Yardley Wood, Birmingham, sent the author a few notes headed *'Memories of New Street,* set down here verbatim. "My father, Harry Leadbetter, born in 1872, worked on old New Street Station for fifty years. He was a foreman shunter on platform one. The glass roof made it seem very warm in summer, especially combined with heat from the engines, etc. The uniform, in those days, was very hot and heavy. He worked six days a week and seven, when his duties included Sundays. No canteen or rest times were allowed; he just had to snatch a meal when and where he could.

"I have no photographs of the station, but remember some of the things my Dad told me . . . Trains were rarely late, especially in the early days, and even if so much as a minute late had to be the subject of a written report.

"Wages for men in my father's grade were paid-out each Tuesday. The cash was not even put in an envelope, just handed over the counter of the pay office.

"Strictly speaking employees and officials were not allowed to leave the station at all while on duty, especially to nip into a pub. They did, of course, and I remember Dad telling me that one day when he had slipped out for a quick one who should he see but the station master with a friend. He was not able to punish or reprimand Dad, as he should not have been there either'.

"Dad brought home to us children, collected from the first class carriages, beautiful, glossy magazines such as the 'Sketch' (not the 'Daily Sketch') and the 'Tatler', also ladies' fashion magazines we should not otherwise have seen. Because of the privilege passes allowed, we were able to go on holiday every year and regularly to London, which was not at all common for working people sixty years ago."

Ex LNER B1 4-6-0, No 61289, *leaving platform 8, for the eastern counties. 29 July 1961.*

M Mensing.

A Mr A.D. McGuirk (aged 85) of Comer, Worcester, wrote concerning New Street when he was a lad, in the days just before the First World War.

"We boys were often thinking of ways to earn a few coppers to help the family budget. One of the ways was to go down to the station entrance near the footbridge to which all the platforms led. We used to wait for passengers who had plenty of luggage and offer to carry it for them, perhaps to the G.W.R. Station at Snow Hill or to the trams. Mind you it was a bit of a struggle for us smaller boys. To overcome the hardship we made small wooden trucks to carry the luggage in. Our good days were on Saturdays and at holiday times... taxis often seemed to be scarce so we provided a useful service for which we earned a few pennies.

"In due course others followed our example and the railway police would not let any of us go on to the footbridge with our hand-trucks, so we had to wait in the porch or arcade. Yet in time they would not let us stay there either, saying we held up the traffic, and turned us away altogether. The travellers had to find an alternative and shortly after this taxis became more frequent. Yet we enjoyed it all while it lasted, and our parents were glad to gain by the enterprise. "

Some interesting stories came from Frank M. Easton of Acock's Green, Birmingham, who wrote an autobiographical booklet, *Stories of my Life on the Railways,* duplicated in a small, private edition, dated 1972.

Frank started his career in January 1918, as a telegraph messenger on the L.N.W.R. at Northampton Station. He was then aged $14^1/_2$ and had just left school. He worked in several different grades and eventually came to New Street, Birmingham, where he served under the newly formed L.M.S. At one period he was an attendant in charge of the special sleeping cars that were attached to ordinary trains and expresses for long distance work. One of these was frequently booked for travel to Inverness by a lady known as the Honourable Mrs Smythe. Others worked through from Bristol to Kingussie for members of the W.D. and H.O. Wills family, renowned as the manufacturers of 'Gold Flake' and 'Woodbine' cigarettes. When New Street offered a regular Friday night sleeping car service to Glasgow, Frank was asked to take charge of the new service. After the 'Royal Scot' engine had been exhibited at New Street Station in 1927, it was transferred to Northampton for further display and Frank accompanied the 'Scot' and its staff train, keeping an eye on things in general and acting as guard.

He was later appointed as one of the first two announcers on the loudspeaker service, installed at the behest of Mr J. Harrison, the then station master, at New Street. At an interview in the S.M.'s office he was told that he had a good speaking voice and that, 'he would do for the job'. Duties were to be shared with a colleague named David Hedges from the parcels department. At 3 p.m. one Saturday the young men were taken to the telegraph office on number one platform and found that part of the building had been partitioned-off and installed with electronic equipment. The S.M. showed them round and how to operate the switchboard, then seated himself in a nearby chair, opened all the switches and boomed-out, "Good afternoon, everybody. This is the station master speaking. The loud-speaker service at New Street is now in operation."

*Ex LMS 'Jubilee' 4-6-0, No
45685 Barfleur, heading the
12.48 pm York - Bristol
Express, passing the remains of
the locomotive turntable with No 5
signalbox on right.
15 April 1961.*

M Mensing.

When asked to take the microphone and say a few words or make an announcement, Frank was so nerve-racked, for fear of making a mistake and disgracing himself in front of his work-mates and the travelling public, that he could think of very little to say. He decided to make a short announcement and picked on the 4.35 p.m. to Adderley Park and Stechford, which was only two stations and short enough by any standards. He made the announcement without fault or delay but remembered as he switched-off that the train in question did not run on Saturdays! It taught him that whatever was said over a microphone had to be correct to the last detail.

At one stage of his duties Frank wondered if he might be mispronouncing some of the place-names, especially those in remote parts of Wales or Scotland. He eventually paid a visit to the B.B.C. headquarters in Broad Street and was able to acquire a series of five small books from them on this teasing subject. When the early services closed at 11 p.m. each evening he would always follow the B.B.C. tradition of saying, "The New Street Loud-Speaker Service is now closing down. Goodnight, everybody—Goodnight". Eventually it was a twenty four hour service, manned in shifts, round the clock.

During the time when the heavy industries section of the British Industries Fair was held at Castle Bromwich and there was considerable traffic arriving for the exhibition, with numerous bewildered visitors — many from overseas — wandering about the station, Frank suggested a special service that was of great value to the enterprise. "A vehicle capable of holding the electronic devices, with a table and seat for the announcer, was stabled in the sidings at Castle Bromwich, giving a loud-speaker service for the duration of the fair". This idea having been accepted, Frank spent a fortnight of each year for the next three years as unofficial host at Castle Bromwich Station. The fair was closed for the duration of the Second World War. "On the platforms were special boards which said — in five languages — 'Alight here for the fair'. I was learning Esperanto at the time and I used to chip in with 'Elpaŝu ĉi tie por las Forio'. Thousands attended the fair each year and it was a wonderful experience for me." Eventually Frank was also in charge of loud-speaker announcements at the station for Bromford Bridge or Birmingham Race course.

At the height of the Second World War Frank claims to have been bombed-out by the first bombs to hit the station. "Blast walls were built round doors and windows, but this was for the blast at ground level. The first bomb burst when it hit the large span roof and most of the grit, dust and soot came over the blast wall and broke my windows. My light went out, the valves went out and everywhere was covered in dust. I was unable to make any announcements but sat there in the semi-darkness as my telephone was the only live one on that side of the station during the air raid. We would get a message from Control such as "Air Raid Message Yellow". This would mean that the announcer kept on the alert and "Air Raid Message Green" would cancel the yellow, but "Air Raid Message Red" was a danger signal and we had to make the following announcement: "Special Announcement — will all passengers please take shelter in the subways." and repeat it two or three times.

"Sometimes we heard the planes or had bombs before we had the red air raid message. Passengers would remain in the subways until the 'All-Clear' was given. After about half an hour, I went down the subway nearest to the office to wait for the All-Clear, and everybody started to laugh at me. I couldn't understand until a woman-guard offered me a mirror: I was covered in soot and dust and looked like a minstrel."

At a later stage in his career Frank gave up announcing and took a post as a train ticket collector. From 1948 until 1968 he spent most of his time on the trains, checking tickets and weeding out fare-dodgers. For a short period he was also a platform ticket collector and advised to seek appointment as an inspector. He realised, however, that the pay was not very much more, but with a great deal more work and responsibility. He was soon back on the rails and remained a travelling collector until his retirement".

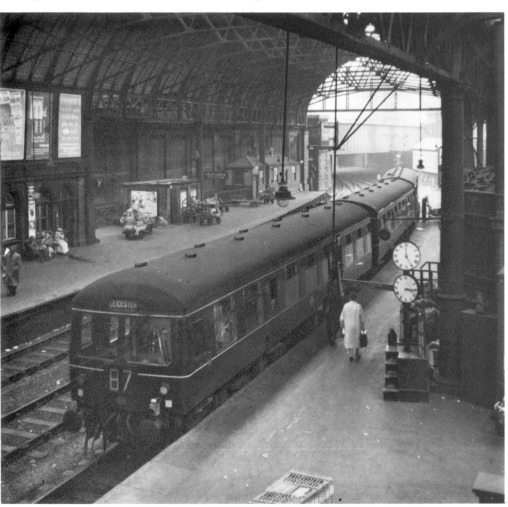

3-car Cravens d.m.u. waiting to leave platform 8 with the 3.15 pm to Leicester. 12 July 1958.

M Mensing.

Mr Percy Braid, of Northfield, worked on the L.N.W.R. side at New Street throughout the First World War, joining the railways shortly after leaving school. He was mainly employed in a junior or trainee capacity, especially in the telegraphic department, until leaving to join the Royal Engineers. Mr Braid's records how the L.N.W.R. staff, although doing their best to co-operate with their M.R. counterparts, normally kept very much to themselves, seldom mixing in off-duty hours. They were all greatly in awe of the station agent, who appears to have out-ranked the station master, at least on the L.N.W.R. side, being responsible to a higher branch of control.

Mr Braid was present when a soldier without a pass or paybook struck a military policeman and escaped arrest by running down the subways and later across the tracks. He also remembers how many of the servicemen mislaid their kit while bidding farewell to friends or family, leaving odd items on platform seats or in the waiting rooms. It was almost a daily chore to collect missing rifles, packs or bayonets and lodge them at the office of the Railway Transport Officer.

In 1917 the branch of the telegraph office in which Percy Braid worked was transferred to a new wing of the Queen's Hotel, perhaps as a wartime measure. Although only a lad-employee, he was sometimes on late duties, shared with a youth of roughly his own age. They took it in turns to have a short break and Percy always spent a few minutes on the bridge or arrival platforms. When an express arrived from London he could often earn a little extra cash, helping people with their luggage, especially as he had to walk back in the direction of the hotel. This was not strictly allowed and he should not have been so far from his post while still on duty. Yet in wartime, with so many staff shortages, his services were greatly appreciated by the travelling public. One evening he offered to carry the case of a smartly dressed stranger, only to discover on reaching the hotel foyer, that this was the hotel manager and a very important person. Percy expected to hear more of this and perhaps get the sack, but nothing was said beyond a mild reproof. In the end things turned out much better than he expected, as he was sent back to a job at platform level where he could greatly increase his slender earnings by part-time portering. He often wondered if there was any connection with the earlier incident.

Mr T.H. Bown of Handsworth has many interesting recollections of his father, whom he was able to identify in newspaper photographs of the 1930s, showing a parade of winning van horse teams in the Queen's Drive, at New Street.

Mr Bown senior worked for the railways in the Birmingham area from the age of fourteen until his retirement at the age of sixty five, commencing an apprenticeship in 1904. He worked in several different grades and eventually became an inspector but was mainly concerned with driving or the care of horses used in the delivery and cartage services. His skills were widely recognised and during the First World War he enlisted in the remount service, frequently taking responsibility for drafts of fresh horses sent from the depots to France and Flanders. Mr Bown appears to have had a way with horses and was able to deal with any troublemakers beyond the control of their normal drivers.

In the school holidays his son would meet him outside the station and ride on the van, not only keeping his father company but helping with deliveries and running errands. Young Bown would wait to join his father's van in Worcester Street, near the southern gateway to the Queen's Drive, dodging the traffic to scramble into the back of the vehicle. He would lie hidden behind a small screen that divided the driving seat from the body of the van until well clear of the station area. During the Christmas period the business folk and shop assistants were often very generous and Mr Bown was frequently given small presents.

The deliveries were not irksome but at some places there were long waits, when the horses became impatient. Some had the habit of swinging their heads about, even when exploring the contents of a nosebag and scratched or battered other vehicles standing nearby, rarely injuring themselves but damaging paintwork and not making for good relations with the manager or owner of the business where deliveries were being made. At the end of the day most horses were glad to return to stables. Both horses and drivers looked forward to the evening meal and relaxation, frequently driving back to the stables in Curzon Street at a smart canter. The empty van would shake and rattle in such a way as to draw more than frowns or remonstrations from any police officers or senior grades of the cartage department who might be watching. There were tram lines in many of the streets, on which the steel-shod wheels slipped and skidded.

Van horse, sketched by the Halesowen artist, A. L. Hammonds, in the Queen's Drive, New Street 1948.

Permission A L Hammonds.

Railway horse, New Street Station. 1948.

102

The rules of Curzon Street stables were different from those in London and some other cities, where the stable staff took complete control once horses and vans returned to their base. Although not responsible for grooming, the drivers had to harness and unharness their charges and see them safely to their stalls. Unlike some of the former stables of the L.N.W.R. and M.R., where horses and drivers were frequently changed, Curzon Street seems to have had a rule of, 'one man and his van boy to one horse'.

At this point it may seem appropriate to quote a letter from The Right Honourable J. Enoch Powell, M.B.E., M.P., writing from the House of Commons. Mr Powell was educated at King Edward's school, overlooking New Street Station, and made frequent use of the trains. He states that, "The principal impact of New Street Station upon King Edward's School while I was there (1925-30) was its contribution to the thick fogs which from time to time made central Birmingham a tolerable imitation of a London peasouper.

"There was also a certain problem with the balls from the fives courts in our playing ground which shared a party wall with the railway station. Until recently a relic of the wire fence was just observable from the London end of Platform One.

"The main social significance of New Street Station, however, was that it provided ready access to the school for boys drawn from a wide area, so efficient were the rail commuter services at that time. I myself, living at King's Norton six miles from the centre of the city, went home for lunch each day and was rarely late for afternoon classes. There was, however, an arrangement whereby, in order to meet the exigencies of the railway timetable, boys were allowed to leave the last class in the morning two, three or even five minutes early (these were known as exeats). Like all those who were educated in it, I shall always regret the destruction of Charles Barry's building which gave distinction to the centre of a city not otherwise of great architectural note."

Harold Parsons, editor of the magazine *The Blackcountryman,* remembers "that long corridor of steam that was the station bridge, as I was taken across as a child. I recall the two-way bustle of people, the hurrying and scurrying up and down the stairs leading to different platforms as one was whisked along amid a sea of legs and feet . . . the noise of footsteps blending into a sound of its own . . . catching a glimpse of destination and directional signs . . . this way for that city, down there for this . . . creating images of magically sounding places, to those who had access down below where engine whistles exchanged greetings.

"The ticket windows at which we stopped betimes . . . stained wood panelling, surely. And the shops on the bridge . . . sweets, tobacco . . . how select they seemed, the chosen few to occupy that prized position.

"Seeing relatives off to far townships from beside coloured enamel signs (not allowed on to the platforms unless travelling — well *me* anyway) . . . hearing snatches of conversation . . . 'every hour' . . . 'change at so-and-so'. Railwaymen being questioned . . . overhead the arched supports of the bridge structure and beyond that a vast roof-span of glass and girders. Being there, in the late 20s, was to be at the very centre of the action.

"Then, years later, home on leave from the Army, coming down the steps in Station Street and seeing jagged ruins of buildings stabbing the night sky."

For the author of this work New Street Station had a special charm. My first awareness of railways was during childhood visits to Handsworth Park, where I was supported on the parapet of a bridge to see trains on a line running through the park. There was even a small station near the bridge, complete with signals, gas lamps and enamelled signs, at which a few passengers, but not many, even in those days, were bold enough to alight. An extension to this interest was being taken to the Queen's Drive at New Street, where carriages and locomotives, a few similiar to those seen in the park, pulled up not only alongside their platforms but as if beside the roadway itself. It was difficult for a child to tell where the pavements ended or the platforms began. In several places there were no barriers between cars, people and the hissing, gleaming but friendly monsters, normally viewed from a distance. Even at Snow Hill the trains had to be reached down long flights of steps, after queuing to buy tickets and passing through barriers. At New Street it was as if the animals at the zoo had become tame and accessible, while the bars of their cages had been removed.

2-car Metro-Cammel d.m.u. waiting to leave platform 11 with the 4.20 pm Redditch. Note 'Crab' 2-6-0 on right, emerging from the back sidings.

M Mensing.

If Snow Hill was a Zoological Gardens, New Street was a Safari Park. It was possible to walk up to a Midland 'Compound' with the same confidence as one might approach a well-loved dog or pony that had almost become a member of the family. It was wise to be careful, as even a family pet or, for that matter, a favourite uncle, needs the dignity of mutual respect. There were, however, fewer restraints to enthusiasm in New Street than at some other stations. The Great Western was always a line that claimed to cater for train spotters and enthusiasts, yet there was often a hint of patronage in their numerous booklets, jig-saws, publicity hand-outs and conducted tours. The staff were loyal and responsible, but guarded their treasures with perhaps too jealous a mind and hand. New Street was, to my 1930s impressions, less efficient and officious but also more friendly and informal especially on the Midland side.

I made my first train journey from New Street in 1931. On this occasion there was an excursion and we went down to London as a family of three generations, filling a compartment but with sufficient space, light and air even in a 'smoker'. The day began at an unholy hour and lasted until well into the evening, yet the train journey itself was the main event. We arrived at New Street with plenty of time to spare and the chance to see many locomotives that brought to life illustrations in railway books and magazines, as though by magic. Everything about the place, from its porters rolling two milk churns at the same time, one in each hand, to its monumental proportions and even its noise, were a treat for any right-minded child.

BR Standard 'Britannia' class 4-6-2, No 70042 Lord Roberts, with empty stock of the 8.20 am ex-Carlisle platform 3. 23 June 1962.

M Mensing

Long before our train arrived I was a confirmed railway enthusiast and was the same during the war years and even during the muddled period of rebuilding. New Street was a place for setting out on exciting journeys and equally a place of joyful home-coming. Something of the same atmosphere, translated to the needs of a different age, has transferred itself to the new station. A glance over the parapet from the Ringway entrance to see the blue and white, electric *'City of Birmingham'* ease its way towards the South Tunnel, is as exciting in its way as a maroon 'Compound' or 'Claughton' grinding-off to a similar destination.

Mr J. Moore of Castle Bromwich remembers being taken to the Queen's Hotel for afternoon tea, on what must have been special occasions. This was during the 1930s when the dignified surroundings made a lasting impression on his schoolboy mind. The polite and attentive waiters were always smartly turned-out in dress suits with starched fronts of such gleaming whiteness that the eyes were almost dazzled by them. Everything was marked with the hotel and railway crests, from the spotless napery to the smallest jam-spoon. Those entering the building were greeted by the salutations and smiles of a burly doorman, to whom everyone might have been a millionaire. Although very near to the bustle of main street and a busy station, walls were near sound-proof and made guests feel remote from the pressures of every-day life.

Sketch by A. L. Hammonds of a Black '5' on the Midland side at New Street Station. 1950.

Permission: A. L. Hammonds.

106

Ernie Genders, a retired engine driver to whom the author is indebted for many interesting facts concerning the old station, offered a glimpse of different realities with his description of early trains bringing commuters from the suburbs. These would be drawing into their platforms long before the coffee was percolating for breakfast at the nearby Queen's Hotel. People were so eager to be on time that carriage doors were flung open long before the trains stopped. Porters and anyone else already on the platforms had to stand well-clear and lookout for themselves. It is a wonder there were not more accidents, even fatalities, especially from the heavy, swinging doors. A train may have been slightly delayed by the weather or signals but few passengers would dare to risk the displeasure of their employers.

Lawrence Hammonds the celebrated Black Country and Birmingham painter of railway and industrial subjects, frequently made use of the old New Street as a convenient sketching ground, especially when he was a student at the Birmingham College of Art. Some of his most attractive studies in the days of steam were made on the ex-Midland side, where the twin-domed roof, set on mighty iron columns, remained much longer than in the North Western part of the station. The spectacular ironwork, often partly shrouded and obscured by clouds of steam, was evocative of many impressionist paintings by the artists Monet, Pissarro and Manet. When it is remembered how many famous artists, from Turner and David Cox (painter of 'The Birmingham Express'), to Frith and Daumier, were inspired by railway subjects, it is surprising that less imaginative people claim to find stations dull or uninteresting. Yet all the main features for which an artist searches may be found in such places, including atmosphere, scale, perspective and brilliant contrasts of light and shade.

Lawrie often drew and painted the patient vanhorses standing in the Queen's Drive, and found them excellent models, used to long periods of waiting yet undisturbed by the noise of traffic, honking of taxis or the whistles of locomotives. With the brakes screwed-down they were unable to wander away, as often happens when drawing animals in the open fields.

A Mrs Creedy of Kitt's Green wrote interestingly of reminiscences concerning her younger days, when she worked in the book and paper stalls run by Messrs Wyman's Limited, at New Street. She had clear memories of the candy stores on the bridge and the dignified tobacconists opposite, the latter known as 'Salmon and Gluckstein's', noted for making and selling pipes of a type smoked by the former Prime Minister, Stanley Baldwin, later Earl Baldwin of Bewdley. The candy stores were renowned for their high-class confectionery, including numerous tall jars of cachou lozenges with oriental pictures and symbols on the labels. These were highly scented and gave the shop a delightful aroma.

Mrs Creedy was full of admiration for the Queen's Hotel, which she described as one of the most impressive and attractive buildings in Birmingham. The uniformed doormen were always models of smartness, combining dignity with good humour.

The early rush hour was the busiest part of the day, with sales of morning papers and the popular weekly magazines such as 'Picture Post', 'The Leader', 'Illustrated' and 'Everybody's', all of which seemed to vanish within a short time, during the late 1950s. People who had mislaid things from items of luggage to elderly aunts frequently made enquiries at the bookstall, tending to treat it not only as a shop but as a combined lost property office and a bureau for missing persons. Mrs Creedy described New Street as a friendly station, especially during the period of the fifties and sixties when so many of the regular passengers and staff seemed to know each other.

One of New Street's long service employees, who retired in 1982, is Mr Bert Smith of Winson Green, Birmingham. Mr Smith starting his career on the railway in 1932 in the days of the L.M.S. Company, signed-on as a van-boy or carboy, working as assistant to the driver of a light delivery van. His work was to deliver parcels within a mile and a half radius of the station. While it was reported in an evening paper, covering his retirement, that he started

Wyman's bookstall on platform 1.
F Easton.

108

work in the days when the horse and cart set a leisurely pace, this was not strictly accurate as the express parcel vans, drawn by swift, good quality horses, moved in and out of main street traffic at an incredible speed. Bert, like other carboys, always travelled in the back of the van, hanging on to a length of knotted rope, ready to jump from the tailboard at a signal from his driver. Life on the railways before the Second World War was still fairly spartan, with none of the "modern comforts and canteen facilities" that came with later years. Yet there was always a spirit of comradeship, especially at New Street.

Over the years Bert Smith worked in several grades and eventually became a supervisor and inspector, acting as host to numerous V.I.P.s and rolling out the red carpets for several members of the Royal Family when they came to Birmingham.

The following notes consist mainly of extracts from a letter by Harry C. Stafford of Station Road, Wythall, whose early interest in railways was centred on the Great Western although he later discovered some of the good things he may well have missed or taken for granted in other regions. "My memories of New Street Station go back to the 1920s when, as a small boy I was taken to stay with relatives at Stoke-on-Trent. At that time the L.M.S. Railway Company had not long been formed so that for a long time we used to refer to the station as the "North Western Section" (Platforms 1, 2 and 3) and the "Midland Section" (Platforms 4, 5 and 6). Incidentally, Platform 2, which was an island platform, was really two separate platforms, trains using the one side being announced as on "Platform 2 facing 1" while those on the other side were announced as "Platform 2 facing 3". The same applied with Platform 5, also an island platform.

"When I first became interested in railway engines around 1930 there were still a number of old L.N.W.R. "Claughtons", "Princes", "Precursors", etc. around, but as I did not take my first train photographs until 1935, and then only of the Great Western Railway (always my first love) so that I never got round to photographing any of these interesting engines, which had virtually all gone by 1946 when I enlarged my horizons to include the L.M.S.

"I do remember my first ride on "The Devonian" in 1938, when I began my summer holiday for that year. Hitherto, I had always gone from Snow Hill to the West Country, but on this occasion, having to work on Saturday morning, I had no option but to go to New Street. "The Devonian" on that occasion was, I seem to recall, drawn double-headed by two Midland "Compounds". The journey impressed me by reason of the fact that at that time, almost as soon as the train had cleared the tunnels, it seemed to be in the country — there was little or no housing to be seen from the line at Northfield or King's Norton, and it remained that way until about 1948.

"On summer Saturdays "The Devonian" eventually missed out New Street, using the line through Brighton Road and King's Heath to rejoin the main line just short of King's Norton. On these occasions passengers from New Street were served by a summer Saturday Holiday Train from Nottingham to Torbay, which called at New Street at 12.46 p.m. instead of "The Devonian's" usual time of 1.39 p.m.

"I really got to know New Street during the Second World War, for not only was this the only route to the West of England, the service from Snow Hill to Bristol being withdrawn "for the duration", but also I travelled regularly on leave from the Forces during 1941 and 1942 when I was stationed in the Orkneys and on the mainland of Scotland. There was one occasion, following air raids on April 9th/10th 1941, when I was coming back from Devon and the train could not get into New Street on one side because of bomb damage, and we had to travel via Kidderminster and Stourbridge Junction into Snow Hill.

"The journeys back to the Orkneys meant we had either to catch the 11.00 train to Carlisle, or the 11.35 to Crewe, then change into the through train to Perth, for a further train on to Thurso. During the winter, the lines beyond Perth were often blocked with snow, which meant that anyone on leave had to wait until trains could get through again, while anyone about to go on leave was, of course, unable to start. Our troop sergeant major, when his leave was due to end, would make enquiries as to whether the line north of Inverness was opened or closed because of snow. When the answer came that the line was closed the T.S.M. got his leave pass stamped, which meant that he could go back home for another day, and this was repeated every day until the snow finally cleared.

"After the war I resumed my contacts with New Street and for a number of years used this line to go down to Bristol for train photography. The last of the old L.N.W.R. engines had by now long gone from the passenger services, but Midland "Compounds" and "0-6-0's" were still in evidence. I think that the last time I saw a "Compound" on "The Devonian" was November 7th 1953, although they continued in fairly large numbers on local services between Birmingham and Derby until about 1959. It was during these last years that I suddenly became aware that they were being withdrawn and disappearing, and photographed everyone I saw. The 0-6-0's lasted for a few years longer, but by 1962 or so they, too, were gone.

"The Queen's Drive holds one particular memory for me, for it was at the far end of the drive by a tobacconist's kiosk that I waited on our first date for the girl who in 1953 was to become my wife. I often found the Queen's Drive exit from New Street much easier, especially when the train arrived on either platform 6 or 7, avoiding the crowds on the footbridge.

"The old New Street Station was often regarded as a relic of the Victorian Age, but it undoubtedly had character and the present station has, to me at any rate, a mausoleum-like atmosphere.

"I think that my last steam-hauled ride out of, or into, New Street, was on Whit-Monday June 7th 1965, when we had a family outing to Matlock and Bakewell, although the train was only steam-hauled as far as Derby and back. Shortly afterwards steam was banned at New Street, and one or two of the railtours that I travelled on later were diesel-hauled from New Street as far as Saltley, when they then changed to steam."

111

New Street Station - 1967.

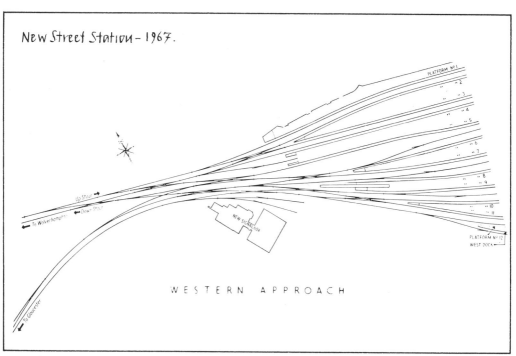

WESTERN APPROACH

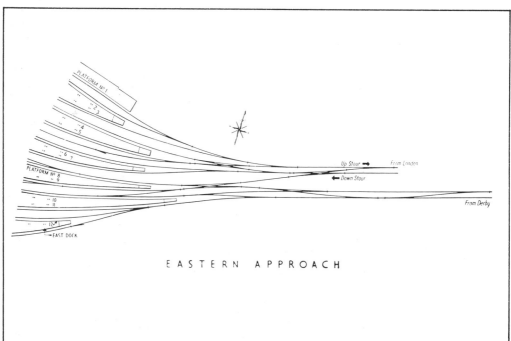

EASTERN APPROACH

The New Station

It was decided to rebuild New Street, during the early 1960s, not only because so much of the old structure, fittings and equipment had become outmoded or outworn, but to harmonise with a completely new concept in railways, of which electrification of the West Coast route and speedier links between Euston and the West Midlands were essential features. It was part of the London, Midland Region's plan for wholesale modernisation that would place it in the forefront of international railway development. Work began on the rebuilding in 1964, and was completed in 1967 at a cost of £4m.

From the early 1960s it was decided to run-down many of the services from Snow Hill and divert them to New Street. This related not only to the important lines to Paddington via Banbury and Leamington, but also trains to Stourbridge and Kidderminster via a reinstated Galton Junction and Smethwick Junction.

However, during the modernisation and electrification of New Street, London services were diverted to Snow Hill. But when Snow Hill finally closed all London services (including Paddington) were transferred to New Street; although Moor Street (ex G.W.R.) services remained unaltered.

Ground plan of New Street 1967.

Permission: British Rail.

South Tunnel on LNWR side line towards Coventry. Line to Derby (Midland tunnel) in foreground. 1966.

F Easton.

As with the old station, the running tracks of modern New Street are below adjacent street levels, their formation being in a cutting that runs roughly south east to north west. In the new building the Queen's Drive was eliminated, covered by extra track and platform space. Floors are of pre-stressed concrete throughout, the upper deck or raft supported from station-level by over 200 columns, resting on piles driven 30ft below ground level. The station area is also the site of a large block of residential flats with twenty one storeys, known as 'Stephenson House' out of deference to the great railway engineers responsible for the London and Birmingham Railway.

Remodelling the building started from the Station Street side and worked—through to the original platform one on the New Street side, thus reversing the plan of development before the grouping. One of the first changes, however, was to drive through a link between the bay-sidings on platform one, to serve as continuous running tracks. The Queen's Hotel was totally demolished, thus depriving Birmingham of one of its better known and more respectable landmarks. Reopening, as the work proceeded, was timed to correspond with the reconstruction of each platform. A great deal of the work was done by private contractors, mainly the firm of C. Bryant and Son (structural work), assisted by British Railways. Birmingham Corporation, while supporting the modernisation scheme in all its phases, did not contribute to the rebuilding but leased part of the site.

116

The Navigation Street bridge, although changed as little as ten years earlier, had to be rebuilt a second time — also raised to make way for overhead wires. The brick pier supporting the centre of the bridge was replaced by concrete box-beams, each 15ft high and 165ft long, weighing 250 tons. During rebuilding, two steamhauled spoil trains removed 600 tons of waste material each day. Travelling steam cranes were borrowed from both Rugby and Willesden Junction, the Willesden crane — in particular — being in immaculate condition — having a freshly painted maroon livery — while the Rugby crane was plain black. Until the completion of the new power box at the north end of the station, the old number five box had to be retained throughout, in daily use.

The new power signal box was one of the more interesting features of the rebuilt New Street, occupying a site roughly the same as the former locomotive turntable. It was brought into operation on the 3rd July 1966, controlling routes not only in the centre of Birmingham but over a wide surrounding area. With other power boxes at Walsall, Coventry and Wolverhampton (all on recently electrified lines), it replaced sixty four manual boxes, controlling eighty five route miles.

Modern Operations.

Unlike its predecessor, the present New Street Station has most of its refreshment rooms, bookstalls and other amenities not on the platforms but in or leading from the main concourse, at street level. There are now, however, small waiting rooms — centrally heated — at platform level, introduced after the opening of the station, to comply with public demand. The ticket office in the passenger concourse, is to the left of the barrier, entering the station from the ringway. It is fully mechanised and automated, with windows relating to destinations in alphabetical order, issuing over 7,500 tickets per day. The installation of the barrier at this level, ended New Street's right to be known as one of the few remaining open stations in Britain.

An all-electric service to London-Euston began with the opening of the new station in 1967. At first it was a (through) hourly service, although later run on an half-hourly schedule. Inter-city expresses with sound-proof windows and air-conditioning, designed on the saloon plan, were eventually scheduled to leave for Euston at 18 and 48 minutes past the hour, capable of reaching 100 m.p.h. This is at least five times the speed of express trains as envisaged by directors of the London and Birmingham Railway Company. Normal journey time to Euston is an hour and a half, centre-to-centre.

In 1972 it was announced that Birmingham, New Street, would be promoted to become a regional headquarters, and the centre of one of eight new 'territories' intended to replace the former five regions and twenty eight divisions of British Rail.

The overall controller of New Street Station, at the time of writing, is Mr I.D. King, known as the Area Manager. Many useful statistics and a brief outline of the modern station and its operations are contained in a leaflet compiled by Mr King, entitled 'Welcome to New Street', from which some of the above facts and figures have been drawn.

117

LNER B1 4-6-0, No 61041, *and*
LMS 'Jubilee' 4-6-0, No 45579
Punjab, *waiting to leave*
platform 9 with the 8.0 am
Newcastle-on-Tyne - Cardiff
train. 18 June 1960.

M Mensing.

Locomotive Notes

These few notes concern some of the more interesting and typical types of motive power seen in or near New Street and on the early London and Birmingham Railway from the 1840s to nationalisation. It is not intended as a complete record but may serve as a guide to further study, also to expand other notes appearing in earlier parts of this book.

The first engines to work on the London and Birmingham Railway, apart from any used by the engineers and contractors, were the so-called Bury-type. These may be classed as 2-2-0's, although the leading wheels were of comparatively large diameter for supporting bogies. They remained in service for a number of years and were mainly stabled at the 'engine house' near Curzon Street Station, or at Vauxhall. Their twin cylinders were 13in x 18in. Wheel base was 6ft 5in.

A frequent and early visitor to New Street, from its time of opening, was *Columbine,* which had the distinction of being the first locomotive to be constructed at Crewe Works. It was designed by Francis Trevithick, son of Richard Trevithick, inventor of the first railway locomotive. It first ran on the Grand Junction Railway. In 1846 it was absorbed into L.N.W.R. stock. It had a 2-2-2 wheel arrangement with inclined outside cylinders of $15^1/_4$in x 20in. Driving wheels were 6ft 3in diameter. Tractive effort was 6,325 lbs. The engine has been preserved and restored at the National Railway Museum, York.

Also dating from this period were certain large engines for both express workings and mixed traffic. These were long-boilered types with six-wheeled tenders, from the Bury Locomotive Works but designed by an engineer named Crampton. They had an unusual wheel arrangement and were classed as (2-2-2)- 2-0. There were six separate, supporting or bogie wheels at the front-end with large diameter driving wheels at the rear. Dimensions of driving wheels were 8ft 4in. Bogies were 4ft 6in. Perhaps the most outstanding and best known of this type was *Liverpool,* named after its place of origin. It frequently worked on main line services between London and Birmingham. Outside cylinders were 18in x 24in. Boiler heating surface was 2,290 square feet and steam pressure 120 p.s.i. Wheel base was $18ft5^3/_4$in. Total weight of engine and tender was 35 tons. It had Stephenson link motion.

Another long-boilered engine was Stephenson's 'A' Type (2-2)-2-0. This was designed by Robert Stephenson and used mainly in the Southern Division of the L.N.W.R. Cylinders were 15in x 24in. Boiler heating surface was 830 square feet, although an even larger version of the same engine had a heating surface of 939.4 square feet. Wheel base was 13ft and total weight 24.2 tons.

Early tank engines widely used in the Birmingham area were 0-4-2s designed by J. Edward McConnell, formerly of the Birmingham and Gloucester Railway, but later Chief Locomotive Engineer for the Southern Division of the L.N.W.R. These engines were mainly used for shunting but often seen on locals, especially on the Lichfield and Sutton Coldfield routes.

During the second half of the 19th century there were many express workings into New Street behind 'Lady of the Lake' Class engines of the L.N.W.R. These were a type designed by John Ramsbottom in 1859, but later rebuilt and greatly improved by F. W. Webb. Wheel arrangement was 2-2-2 with 7ft 9in driving wheels and two 16in x 24in outside cylinders. Boiler pressure was 140lbs p.s.i., with a tractive effort of 7,850lbs. Total weight of engine and tender was 56 tons 7 cwts. These engines frequently averaged 64 m.p.h., between Watford and Rugby.

There were several locomotives with the sobriquet of 'Jumbos', working for three or four main line companies. Those on the L.N.W.R. were perhaps the best known, officially belonging to the 'Precedent' Class, powerful and hard-working for both size and modest appearance. They were 2-4-0s with 6ft 9in driving wheels, designed by F. W. Webb and appearing from 1874. Cylinders were 17in x 24in. Boiler pressure was 150 p.s.i. and tractive effort 10,918 lbs. Weight was 60 tons 12 cwts for engine and tender. 'Jumbos' frequently handled the two-hourly expresses between New Street and Euston but were eventually replaced by the 'Precursors'. Many were still on active service with the L.M.S. some time after the grouping of 1923.

The first locomotive to run between London and Birmingham in two hours, on an experimental basis, was No. 1960 *Frances Stephenson,* a compound locomotive of the 'Alfred the Great' Class. This had been designed by F.W. Webb in 1901, being a 4-4-0 with two high pressure cylinders of 16in x 24in and two low pressure cylinders of $20^1/_2$in x 24in. Driving wheels were 7ft 1in diameter. Boiler pressure was 175 lbs and tractive effort 13,229 lbs. Total weight was 82 tons 12 cwts. It completed its test run of 113 miles in 115 minutes, non-stop.

Two-hourly services were also handled by the powerful 4-6-0 'Prince of Wales' Class, engines first appearing in 1911. Over 230 of these were built at Crewe, many still appearing in daily service after the grouping.

Early locomotives of the Midland Railway appeared in green liveries. They were often 0-6-0 tender engines with either straight or curved outside frames, although the curved type was less frequently seen in the Birmingham area. These latter were mainly built by Dubs and Company for the M.R. and used in a wide range of passenger workings and mixed traffic. On the whole Midland types were fairly small engines and frequently worked trains by means of double-heading.

The Johnson single 4-2-2 locomotive was frequently seen at New Street until the 1920s, sometimes acting as a pilot to 0-6-0s and other types. These engines appeared in four main groups. The last or fourth group, which was also the most powerful, had driving wheels with a diameter of $7ft9^1/_2$in. They ran swiftly and silently and were widely known as 'Spinners'.

A considerable part of express passenger workings on the Midland, during the second half of the 19th century, was handled by Johnson 4-4-0s. These were produced in fairly large numbers at the Derby works, between 1876 and 1901. Swift and reliable their design — in aesthetic terms — was one of the most attractive to appear at New Street.

The Standard Midland Compound was a fine engine of its type, frequently transferred from the north eastern to the Euston run, shortly after the grouping. There seems to have been no particular reason for this as the 'Georges' and 'Precursors', formerly at the disposal of the L.N.W.R., were almost equally good, some might think better. It showed, however, the predominance of the Midland faction over the L.N.W.R. group, at the time of amalgamation. The Midland 'Compound' was a three cylinder engine, of 4-4-0 wheel arrangement, designed by W.S. Johnson at the Derby works in 1905. It was modified and brought up-to-date by R.M. Deeley in 1914, having a single high pressure and twin low pressure cylinders. The high pressure cylinder was internal. Diameter of driving wheels was 7ft. Boiler pressure was 220 lbs p.s.i. and tractive effort 24,024 lbs. Total weight was 105 tons 16 cwts. Engine No. 1000 of the Midland Railway has been preserved at York and is one of the engines still available for special running. It returned to New Street on the 30th August 1959, refurbished in its Midland livery, at the head of a Stephenson Locomotive Society Special. Engines of this type were fairly ubiquitous on the M.R. and later in all parts of the L.M.S. system, although seldom appearing on the Gloucester line, south of Birmingham, until the late 1930s.

As trains grew longer and heavier the Midland 'Compounds' were in turn replaced by 'Class 5' engines of 4-6-0 wheel arrangement, such as the 'Claughtons' and the 'Patriots', especially on the two-hourly Euston run. The 'Claughtons' were a famous class designed by C.J. Bowen-Cooke of the L.N.W.R. in 1913. They were well-balanced engines and much steadier for the crew on the footplate than the swaying, hunting 4-4-0s. They had four cylinders of $15^{3}/_{4}$in x 26in and a tractive effort of 23,683 lbs. Weight of engine and tender was 118 tons 10 cwts. Many of the 'Claughtons' were rebuilt by Sir Henry Fowler as the 'Patriot' Class, later known as 'Baby Scots', with increased boiler pressure and tractive effort, but retaining many of their original features, especially the wheels. The duties of the 'Patriots' and 'Claughtons' were eventually shared by the 'Jubilee' Class of Sir William Stanier — with its tapered boiler, some eventually having double chimneys — which came in during the early 1940s. 'Jubilees' were said to be an improved or extended version of the 'Patriots'. Boiler pressure was 225 lbs p.s.i. Cylinders were 17in x 26in and tractive effort 26,610 lbs. Neither must we forget the frequent incursions into New Street of Stanier's ubiquitous and most-famous workhorse of all, the 4-6-0 L.M.S. 'Black 5s'.

B.R. Standard 'Class 5' locomotives were found to be a useful post war type in the London Midland Region and frequently worked into New Street. These were designed for British Railways by R.A. Riddles. They weighed 123 tons 4 cwts, with a tractive effort of 26,120 lbs.

The first diesel-hauled trains came in 1953. These were at first confined to the former L.N.W.R. side and included visits from the prototype ex-L.M.S. No. 10000 (built at Derby in 1947), mainly on workings to and from Euston.

The first light-weight diesel multiple-unit was a 'B.I.F.' special, running in March 1953. This was a twin car set powered by two 150 h.p. diesel engines, taking ten minutes for the journey from New Street to Castle Bromwich, its top speed being 62 m.p.h. The driver was Leonard Beard of Derby. The first regular D.M.U. service to Lichfield was in 1954, while the last steam-hauled local ran, via Sutton Coldfield, on 3rd March 1956.

[162]

London and Birmingham Railway.

TIME TABLE.

NOTICE. The time is that of the **Arrival** of the Trains, and Passengers, to ensure their being booked, should be at the PRINCIPAL STATIONS **five minutes** earlier, and at the INTERMEDIATE STATIONS **ten minutes** earlier.

Carriages intended to receive Passengers who are expected by the Trains at the London or Birmingham Stations, should be on the Arrival Side of such Stations, a quarter of an hour, at least, before the time specified in the Tables.

Distance from Euston Station.	LONDON to BIRMINGHAM. STATIONS.	Down Trains.													Sunday Trains.				
		6 A.M. Mixed *†‡‖	7 A.M. Third Class	8 A.M. Mixed	8¾ A.M. First Class *§†	9¼ A.M. Mixed to Rug. ‖‡	9¾ A.M. Mail. 1st Cl. *§	11 A.M. Mixed *‡‖	2 P.M. Mixed †	3 P.M. Mixed to Aylesbury.	5 P.M. Mixed ‖	6 P.M. Mixed to Wolverton	8½ P.M. Mail Mixed *§	9 P.M. Mail ‖‡	8 A.M. Mixed ‡‖	9¾ A.M. Mail 1st Cl. *§	6 P.M. Mixed to Wolverton.	8½ P.M. Mail Mixed *§	9 P.M. Mail ‖‡
Miles		H. M.	H. M.	H. M.	H. M.	H. M.	H. M.	H. M.	H. M.	H. M.	H. M.	H. M.	H. M.	H. M.	H. M.	H. M.	H. M.	H. M.	H. M.
—	Leave LONDON at	6. 0	7. 0	8. 0	8.45	9.15	9.45	11. 0	2. 0	3. 0	5. 0	6. 0	8 30	9. 0	8. 0	9.45	6. 0	8.30	9. 0
11½	Arrive at HARROW	—	7.42	8 29	—	—	—	—	2.29	3.29	5.29	6.29	—	—	8.32	—	6.29	—	—
17¾	WATFORD	6.46	8. 2	8.47	—	—	—	11.47	2.47	3.47	5.47	6.47	--	—	8.51	—	6.47	—	—
21	KINGS LANGLEY	—	8.17	8.57	—	—	—	—	—	3.57	—	6.57	—	—	9. 1	—	6.57	—	—
24½	BOXMOOR	—	8.32	9. 7	—	—	—	—	3. 7	4. 7	—	7. 7	—	—	9.12	—	7. 7	—	—
28	BERKHAMPSTEAD	—	8.47	9.19	—	—	—	—	3.19	4.19	—	7.19	—	—	9.25	—	7.19	—	—
31¾	TRING	7.21	9. 1	9.31	10. 8	10.36	11. 3	12.24	3.31	4.31	6.21	7 31	9.49	10.11	9 36	11. 3	7.31	9.49	10.11
43½	AYLESBURY	—	—	10.15	—	—	—	—	—	5.15	—	8.15	—	—	10.15	—	8.15	—	—
41	LEIGHTON	7.41	9.36	9.51	—	—	—	12.44	3.51	—	6.40	7.51	—	—	9.56	—	7.51	—	—
46½	BLETCHLEY (& Fenny Stratford)	—	9.56	10. 6	—	—	—	—	4. 6	—	—	8. 5	—	—	10.12	—	8. 6	—	—
52½	WOLVERTON	8. 7	10.10	10.20	10.55	11.22	11.47	1.11	4.20	—	7. 5	8.30	10.35	10.55	10.25	11.47	8.30	10.35	10.55
60	ROADE	—	10.40	10.49	—	—	—	—	4.49	—	7.34	—	—	—	10.55	—	—	—	—
62¾	BLISWORTH	8.42	12.30	10.58	—	11.55	12.20	1.48	4 58	—	7.42	—	11. 8	11.25	11. 7	12.20	—	11. 8	11.25
69¾	WEEDON	8.59	12.49	11.17	11.51	12.12	12.36	2. 7	5.17	—	8. 1	—	11.26	11.42	11 26	12.36	—	11.26	11.42
75½	CRICK (and Welton)	—	1. 9	11.35	—	—	—	—	5 35	—	—	—	—	—	11.46	—	—	—	—
83	RUGBY (Mid.Cs.Jn.)	9.30	1.28	11.56	--	1. 0	1. 8	2.43	5.56	—	8.38	—	11.58	12.15	12. 5	1. 8	—	11.58	12.15
89	BRANDON	—	1.48	12.13	—	—	—	—	6.13	—	—	—	—	—	12.25	—	—	—	—
94	COVENTRY	9.57	2. 2	12.26	12.52	—	1.34	3.12	6.26	—	9. 2	—	12.27	—	12.40	1.34	—	12.27	—
103	HAMPTON (Derby Junc.)	10.25	2.36	12 55	1.21	—	—	—	6.55	—	—	—	—	—	1.15	—	—	—	—
112½	BIRMINGHAM about	11½	3¼	1¼	2	—	2¼	4¼	7½	—	10¼	—	1¼	—	2	2½	—	1¼	—

Distance from Birmingham.	BIRMINGHAM to LONDON. STATIONS.	Up Trains.													Sunday Trains.				
		Mixed from Wolverton.	7 A.M. Mixed	Mixed from Aylesbury.	8½ A.M. Mail 1st Cl. *§	10 A.M. Mixed †‖	12 NOON Mixed *	1¼ P.M. Mixed *†	Mixed from Rugby. ‡‖	2⅓ P.M. Third Class	4 P.M. First Class *§	6 P.M. Mixed. ‖‡	12 P.M. Mail Mixed *§	1 A.M. from Rugby ‖‡	Mixed from Wolverton.	8½ A.M. Mail. 1st Cl. *§	1½ P.M. Mixed. ‡*‖	12 P.M. Mail Mixed. *§	1 A.M. from Rugby ‖‡
Miles		H. M.	H. M.	H. M.	H. M.	H. M.	H. M.	H. M.	H. M.	H. M.	H. M.	H. M.	H. M.	H. M.	H. M.	H. M.	H. M.	H. M.	H. M.
—	LEAVE BIRMINGHAM at	—	7. 0	--	8.30	10. 0	12. 0	1.15	—	2.20	4. 0	6. 0	12. 0	—	—	8.30	1.30	12. 0	—
9¼	ARRIVE AT HAMPTON (Derby Junc.)	—	7.20	--	—	10.20	12.20	1.35	—	2.54	4.20	6.19	—	—	—	—	1.51	—	—
18¾	COVENTRY	—	7.47	--	9.12	10.47	12.47	2. 4	—	3.29	4.47	6.45	12.47	—	—	9.12	2.17	12.47	—
23¼	BRANDON	—	8. 5	--	—	—	1. 5	—	—	3 47	—	7. 3	—	—	—	—	2.35	—	—
29¼	RUGBY (Mid.Cs.Jn.)	—	8.23	—	9.43	11.17	1.23	2.35	4. 0	4.13	5.17	7.18	1.23	1. 5	—	9.43	2.53	1.23	1. 5
37	CRICK (and Welton)	—	8.50	—	—	—	1.50	—	—	4.41	—	7.42	—	—	—	—	3.20	—	—
42¾	WEEDON	—	9. 4	—	10.18	11.54	2. 4	3.11	4.31	5. 4	5.54	7.56	2. 4	1.40	—	10.18	3.34	2. 4	1.40
49¾	BLISWORTH	—	9.27	—	—	12.16	2.28	3.35	4.55	5.28	6.16	8.17	2.28	2. 0	--	—	3.58	2.28	2. 0
52¼	ROADE	—	9.35	—	—	—	2.38	—	—	5.37	—	8.27	—	—	—	—	4. 8	—	—
59¾	WOLVERTON	6.45	9.55	—	11. 5	12.40	3. 0	4. 0	5.20	6.15	6.40	8.45	2.55	2.30	6.45	11. 5	4.30	2.55	2.30
65¾	BLETCHLEY (& Fenny Stratford)	6.58	10.21	—	—	—	3.26	—	—	6.37	—	9.11	—	—	6.58	—	4.56	—	—
71¼	LEIGHTON	7.14	10.37	—	—	1.16	3.42	—	—	6.58	7.16	9.26	—	—	7.14	—	5.12	—	—
	Leave AYLESBURY for LONDON	7. 0	—	11. 0	—	—	—	—	--	—	7. 0	—	—	—	7. 0	—	5 0	—	—
80¼	TRING	7.41	11. 4	11.26	12. 6	1.42	4.11	5. 0	6.21	7.30	7.42	9.51	4. 1	3.35	7.41	12. 6	5.41	4.1	3.35
84½	BERKHAMSTEAD	7.54	11.16	11.39	—	—	4.25	—	—	8.12	—	10. 3	—	—	7.54	—	5.54	—	—
87¾	BOXMOOR	8. 4	11.25	11.49	—	—	4.34	—	—	8.27	—	10.12	—	—	8. 4	—	6. 4	—	—
91¼	KINGS LANGLEY	8.12	—	11.57	—	—	—	—	—	8.37	—	—	—	—	8.12	—	6.12	—	—
94¾	WATFORD	8.21	11.40	12. 7	—	2.11	4.49	—	—	8.47	8.11	10.27	—	—	8.21	—	6.21	—	—
100¾	HARROW	8.39	11.55	12.24	—	—	5. 7	—	—	9. 7	—	10.42	—	—	8.39	—	6.39	—	—
112½	LONDON about	9¼	12¼	1½	1¼	3¼	6	6¼	8	10	9½	11¼	5¼	5	9¼	1¼	7¼	5¼	5

N.B.—The times of the Trains conveying the Mails are fixed by the Postmaster General, under the powers granted by Act of Parliament, Act 1 & 2 Vic. cap. 98.

* Trains in conjunction with the Grand Junction, Liverpool and Manchester.
† Trains in conjunction with the Birmingham and Derby Junction.
‡ Trains in conjunction with the North Midland.
§ Trains in conjunction with the North Union, and Lancaster and Preston Junction.
‖ Trains in conjunction with the Midland Counties, Leicester, Nottingham, and Derby.

Waiting Rooms, with Female Attendants, are provided at the Euston, Watford, Wolverton, Rugby, Coventry, and Birmingham Stations: Refreshments at Wolverton and Birmingham.

Private Carriages and Horses cannot be booked unless they are at the Stations fifteen minutes before the time above specified; nor can they be conveyed by the Night Mail Trains up or down, nor by the down Day Mail Train.

Carriages, Trucks, and Horse Boxes are kept at all the Principal Stations; but to prevent the possibility of disappointment, it is requisite that one day's previous notice be given whenever they are required.

The Company will only hold themselves responsible for Luggage when it is booked and paid for, according to its value; and they strongly recommend to Passengers to have their Name and Destination in all cases distinctly marked thereon, and to satisfy themselves that it is deposited on the Company's Carriages.

Post Horses, for the conveyance of Carriages arriving at the Euston Station, are always in readiness, at a charge of 10s. 6d., including Post-boy, to any part of London.

1st JUNE, 1841.

[See over.]

Smith and Ebbs, Printers, Tower-hill, London.

Timetable for the London and Birmingham Railway, June 1841.

'Waiting Rooms with Female Attendants, are provided at the Euston, Watford, Wolverton, Rugby, Coventry and Birmingham Stations. Post Horses for the conveyance of Carriages are always in readiness, at a charge of 10s 6d, including Post-boy, to any part of London'.

New Street Tunnels

New Street Station is approached by rail through seven tunnels. The longest of these is the north tunnel which is on the former Stour Valley line and handles traffic to Wolverhampton and points north. It is 760 yards in length with a rising gradient of 1 in 100 towards Wolverhampton. Although frequently recorded as the Monument Lane Tunnel, this is not its official title and seldom used by railwaymen.

The second longest is the south tunnel, serving traffic for both Euston and Derby. It is 266 yards long, rising at 1 in 53 but with a short section of 1 in 50. Trains were frequently stuck or stranded in the south tunnel if anything affected their momentum.

Canal Tunnel, in a westward direction, is 224 yards long, running under part of the Birmingham Canal Navigation system, which it serves as a form of aqueduct. The interior tends to be damp and murky, for which a certain amount of unavoidable seepage is partly responsible. The rising gradient is 1 in 80.

Bath Road Tunnel is 209 yards long on a westwards rising gradient of 1 in 80.

Holliday Street Tunnel, on the west suburban route, is 93 yards long at 1 in 80.

The shortest tunnel is Granville Street, at 81 yards in length, on a gradient of 1 in 80, this being a borderline case between a bridge and a tunnel.

Acknowledgements

Mr Bryan Holden. The Librarian and Staff of Birmingham Central Library. The Librarian and Staff of Harborne Library. The Editor and Staff of the *Birmingham Evening Mail*. Mr Harold Parsons (Editor of *The Black Countryman*). Mr I. D. King (Area Manager, New Street Station). Mr G.E. Hughes and the Staff of Stanier House, B.R. Mr M. Mensing. Mr C. Chadwick. Mr Michael Williams. Mr W.A. Camwell. The Rt. Hon. J. Enoch Powell M.B.E., M.P. The Staff of the National Railway Museum, York. Mr A.L. Hammonds, A.R.C.A., R.B.S.A. Mr F. Easton. Mr G.R. Moyle. Mr F. Hubball. Mr T. Nicholls. Mrs U.M. Bradbury. Mr J. Moore. Mr B.E. Timmins. Mr E. Tomlinson. Mr Harry C. Stafford. Mr T.N. Bown. Mrs Creedy. Mr Percy Braid. Mr F.A. Jones. Mr E. Genders. Mrs A. Kellett. Mr L. Clifford. Mr R.S. Potts. Mr A.D. McGuirk. Mr R. Hollins. The Westwood Press.

Donald J. Smith has written twenty books on various aspects of transport history, including railways, canals and horse-drawn vehicles.

Born in Birmingham in 1927, he was educated at Tamworth Grammar School, and attended Stourbridge College of Art and the University College of Cardiff.

Married with two sons, he still resides locally. His interests include the graphic arts, the study of transport history and architecture.

A companion volume:
'Salute to Snow Hill'

Birmingham had two major railway stations up to 1977. *Salute to Snow Hill* is a tribute to that other station, now sadly no more, but for some 125 years a foremost GWR station.

Written by Derek Harrison, it is well illustrated with many early photographs.

Now in its fourth edition, the book is a requiem rather than an official history — penned for those who want to remember . . . and for those who will never forget.

Published by Barbryn Press Ltd.